THINK.
INNOVATE.
CREATE.

SHARPEN YOUR VISION, FIND EFFECTIVE STRATEGIES AND MAXIMIZE YOUR INFLUENCE

DR. APRIL RIPLEY

**DREAM
RELEASER**
ENTERPRISES

Think. Innovate. Create.
Sharpen Your Vision, Find Effective Strategies and Maximize
Your Influence

by Dr. April Ripley

copyright ©2020 Dr. April Ripley
ISBN: 9781950718238
Printed in the United States of America

cover design by Kiryl Lysenko
Think. Innovate. Create. is available in Amazon Kindle, Barnes & Noble Nook and Apple iBooks.

THINK.
INNOVATE.
CREATE.

If you are a person of faith and your life's purpose has led you into the world outside of the "church", then this book is for you. In this book, April tells her journey as a businesswoman, while sharing important insights and principles we all can apply and incorporate into our own life's journey.

— *Myles Munroe Jr.*
Chairman, International Third World Leaders Association (ITWLA); President, Munroe Global; Co-founder, Myles and Ruth Munroe Foundation

The author has written with casual precision. The text appeals to our rational and analytical minds with profound psychological constructs. Dr. Ripley presents with an air of intuitive certainty as if her arguments are validated by her own existential convictions. Dr. April Ripley readily appeals to us all to activate the latent power of the mind and its capacity, which is inherently endowed by the Creator Himself, to think, innovate, and create. It is a must-read for all generations.

—*Dr. C. B. Peter Morgan*
Post Graduate Dean of Studies
Caribbean Nazarene College
Trinidad and Tobago

Dr. Ripley has shown gifting as a marketplace consultant. In this book, she shares the keys and principles of leadership she has learned from exemplary leaders. The strategic steps to great leadership and the practical lessons provided in this book are bound to give you the encouragement and push you need to elevate your professional and personal vision and purpose.

—*Ms. Charisa Munroe*
Co-Founder and President
The Myles and Ruth Munroe Foundation

In *Think. Innovate. Create.*, April exegetes principles from ancient texts on vision, strategy, and leadership that will impact your professional and personal lives and increase your potential to change the world for the better.

—*Ronald A. Feinman, DMD*
Founding Member of the American Academy of
Cosmetic Dentistry

Dr. April Ripley's new book marks a significant intervention and an exclamation point in the narrative concerning successful business strategies. This book, linking time-tested and time-honored principles with breakthrough revelations, increases the reader's domain and his or her sphere of operation and responsibility, as effectively as it provides the inner capacity to facilitate one's practice of his or her innate dominion gifts. I recommend its reading by all emerging and functioning leaders born for successful impact in this present global crisis.

—C. Patricia Morgan, PhD
Educational Psychologist and Specialist in Education
and Professional Studies
Author, Consultant
Board Chairperson, University of Fort Lauderdale

In a business world where man has failed nature, Dr. Ripley provides a wise and powerful guide to unlocking creativity and achieving real fulfillment in business. A must-read for anyone who wants to create wealth ethically and leave a lasting legacy.

—Mpume Mabuza
Chairperson
Morgan Advanced Materials

Readers should be advised that this is not another echo but in fact the dispensing of sage, insightful wisdom forged over years of study in the Word of God and through the refining processes of personal experience. Dr. Ripley is among a rare fraternity of Kingdom-oriented stateswomen who understand the times and what the collective of believers ought to do. In this exciting book, Dr. Ripley inspires and challenges us with relevant and practical applications to ensure the fulfillment of God's purpose and vision for our lives.

—Apostle Oscar and Daphne Hoffmeester
Founders and Pastors
Victory Kingdom Church International
Business Consultants

In *Think. Innovate. Create.,* April dives deep into scripture to extract practical insight that every person can use to turn his or her purpose into profit. As a fourth generation entrepreneur, I understand the importance of staying at the cutting edge of innovation and creativity, which makes the difference between mediocre or outstanding generational success and influence.

—Jewel Tankard
Founder and CEO, The Millionairess Club
Star of "Chatter" on FOX Soul
Wife of Gospel Jazz Legend, Ben Tankard

Dr. April Ripley is a Kingdom ambassador whom I have seen grow by applying the principles of faith to everyday living. In this book, she shares that we are designed for a purpose, created to make a difference and take the lead with our inherent giftings on planet Earth. *Think. Innovate. Create.* is another masterpiece by Dr. April that will help you take your faith to a new dimension of life with tangible results. As you read it, get ready to journey into impactful living!

—*J. D. Modede*
Leadership Consultant
Flying High Consulting, Ltd.

Dr. April is not just interested in "God on Sundays" but wants her daily walk and environment to reflect Christ and the Kingdom of God at all times. Her passion is to help people live their fullest lives. In *Think. Innovate. Create.*, she shares sage, practical keys and insights you can apply to your business and personal life. Success begins with wisdom, and it would be wise to read this book.

—*Lewis and Penny Semashkewich*
President, Melewka Structures and Design
Owner, Penny's Headquarters Hair and Day Spa

The first time I met Dr. Ripley, the word *honourable* aptly articulated her personality. This book addresses the essence of our being here on earth, our mandate, our responsibility as stewards over God's earth and creation. In *Think. Innovate. Create.*, Dr. April articulates with clarity and simplicity her understanding and insight of the subject matter. In fact, I have come to know her as a Kingdom ambassador. Everything she does is inspired and motivated by fulfilling the Kingdom mandate and living it out. I can safely say that is her purpose. This book speaks to generations and is a timely reminder that we have a responsibility to take care of creation productively and purposefully.

—John Hafeni Kamati
Founder, JHK Enterprises, CEM

This book displays the creative force of Dr. April Ripley. Her thoughtful and compassionate approach to people and everything she does shines through the text of this book. Her international philanthropic work, strong faith, and commitment to creating a legacy of better lives for all is the essence of who she is and how she leads by example. Leaders around the world should turn to this publication as a practical compendium to learn how to live richer and fuller lives through faithful service, empathy, and true understanding of self-love and the love of others and what it means to be effective and powerful leaders.

—Karen Gamba
Founder and CEO

Ellipsis, LLC, and Against the Current
Co-Founder, ExV Agency
Co-Visionary Women Building Women
Filmmaker, Blue Jay Pictures

Dr. April Ripley is an outstanding source of inspiration for those in the corporate world. The author awakens our imagination, feeds our inspiration, and facilitates the flow of new creative ideas through her work and her life. I encourage you to dive deeper into this work. God has given the vision and strategies to a woman who has vast experience in making dreams reality. Dr. April is a beacon of perseverance, hard work, and integrity. I highly encourage you to take hold of the fundamental principles that she has shared in this book and see how God will use them to transform your life.

—Dr. Reynaldo Franco Aquino and Rev. Miguelina
Baez de Franco
Bishop, PCJC
President, COAPIN
Senior Pastor and Senior Leader, ICRA
Clinical Psychologist and Family Therapist
Co-Founder, FBA Consulting Group

I stand in awe of April's care to grow others from the inside out, both as writer and teacher. This eloquent and invaluable book glows with inner light and practical wisdom that will take you, the reader, on a transformational journey in knowing thyself. It is a gem that is a must-read!

—Ipupa Kasheeta
Founder, IpupaK GrowYou

Dr. April Ripley is a global leader who has stepped up to play a role in addressing issues that humanity grapples with in the twenty-first century. She leads from the front on global diplomatic matters. She is a dynamic, principled, adaptable, and relevant leader in the global village.

—George Mosena
Founder and Chairman, Senapelo
Consulting Engineers
Senior Pastor, House of Faith Christian Centre

Dr. April has high regard for her faith, family, and others. She is talented, creative, and well-versed in life and business, in part because of her desire to educate herself through learning and experiencing various cultures through her travels, locally and abroad. April's desire to build bridges of understanding between cultures is a reflection of her inner care and compassion for others.

—Rachael Karp Rosenberg
Business Consultant

Having partnered with Dr. Ripley on many projects across the globe, I have witnessed this tremendous gift operate in her ambassadorial role, impact the globe, connect with world leaders, and facilitate change wherever she goes. It is a great honor to call Dr. April a faithful co-laborer on the African continent. Her impact is immense, and I have no doubt that this latest project will have the necessary impact our world desperately needs.

—Dr. Maxwell Holland
CEO and Founder, Kingdom Life Embassy
CEO and Founder, 4 Change Organization

As a highly determined and self-motivated marketplace leader and entrepreneur, Ambassador April M. Ripley presents to the reader that there is a purpose for creation, and all are created with the capacity within them to lead and fulfill that specific purpose for their creation. *Think. Innovate. Create.* will empower you with strategies for your own personal mastery and leadership development. Dr. April challenges us to pursue our leadership gifts so we can add value to humanity. Her mentorship by her parents and by world-renowned leader Dr. Myles Munroe, who caused our paths to cross, is evident.

—Charlie Masala
Founder, Zoe Business Consulting
CEO, Myles Munroe International
(Munroe Global)—Africa

If you want to experience breakthroughs and enjoy greater success, then read this book. The strategies and concepts shared are practical yet life-changing.

—Bob Harrison
"Dr. Increase"
President Harrison International

Dr. Ripley's latest publication, *Think. Innovate. Create.*, deftly interweaves principles, strategies, and business models drawn from the biblical text that are key to professional and personal success. Whether employed or self-deployed, this is a must-read for everyone!

—Dr. Lucile Stephens Richardson
Author and Curriculum Consultant

For almost two decades, I have watched April work with grace, dignity, and compassion as a business leader, woman of faith, and overall community servant. Her voice picks up where the elders of the civil and human rights movements left off and is a moral compass for this generation.

—Daniel Blackman
Author, Nationalism Without Compassion

DEDICATION

To my fellow global change agents...
be the change you seek.

Learning expands great souls.

—African proverb

CONTENTS

FOREWORD

In the time that I've known Dr. April Ripley, I've come to appreciate her communication skills, her commitment to socioeconomic empowerment of leaders, and her desire for business success. These three qualities make her uniquely qualified to write *Think. Innovate. Create.*

Although many authors have proficiency in their subject matter, few have actually experienced or cultivated success within their area of proficiency. Dr. April Ripley has both expertise and proficiency in applying the strategies she presents in this book—strategies that have helped her create a sturdy track record of accomplishments—strategies from which you are sure to benefit.

Think. Innovate. Create. provides a practical blueprint for helping you implement and live out the transformational habits that April has researched and recognized to be prevalent among many of the world's top innovators and humanitarian leaders.

Furthermore, I believe you will appreciate the unique mixture of business wisdom and biblical concepts in this book; you will realize a multitude of timeless principles that will inject solutions into your endeavors and organizations. The concepts discussed here are useful because they are based on God's infallible promises. The contents of this book will no doubt change your thought patterns, stretch your capacity, and fortify your vision.

I cannot fathom a better approach for today's generation than a book that combines the timeless wisdom of God with the successes of one who has researched the application of these principles in the lives of the greatest change catalysts of our time, while also applying these principles to her own life and working with a strong sense of urgency to share them with others.

As you journey through the book, your goal will not be merely to get through each chapter, but rather to glean practical application from every page. I pray that you will quickly apply what you learn, as it has the potential to dramatically transform both your business and personal life.

I cannot emphasize enough the timeliness of Dr. Ripley's literary installment. As the world is seeking biblically-based leadership more than ever before in all sectors of society, we have an opportunity to beam a brighter light of moral and ethical character, capability, and compassion into our businesses, families, and communities.

Think. Innovate. Create. could very well be the resource that will usher you into a new dimension and realm—one that allows you to become one of the foremost leaders in your discipline, field, and industry. As you devote your time to absorbing the long-overdue and significant insights within this book, I pray that God will give you a greater understanding of His plans for you as a catalyst for change in the world.

—Dr. N. Cindy Trimm
Life Strategist, Thought Leader, Global Influencer

PREFACE

More than a decade ago, I launched my consultancy, The Premiere Image, Inc. What began as "just me" had evolved into a corporation.

For me, this transition came with a mix of excitement and apprehension. It wasn't a fear of starting; it was the thrill of something new—something planned paired with the recognition of possibilities outside my control. Perhaps I might choose to veer off the plan a bit, follow a trend, and end up who knows where! The new and uncharted realms of entrepreneurship beckoned, and I followed.

Being a person of faith, I read the Bible. I follow the sage words of men and women whose stories tell poignant truths about life, relationships, courage, vision, and much more. Such truths, I believe, can allow me to discover all I seek when it comes to wisdom and wealth.

Sometimes when one hears the word *wealth*, one imagines ultra-rich individuals who have garages full of cars and multiple homes. However, what about wealth that builds schools, provides clean drinking water, builds homes for orphans, and pays for scholarships for those seeking higher education? What about the humanitarians and philanthropists who better humanity? Yes, this is certainly the end result of my desire for wisdom and wealth.

At the outset of my entrepreneurial journey, I wondered if God approved of business. After all, very little was being said about the marketplace in church. It was as if we attended church on Sundays, and then Monday through Friday we had to wing it. This didn't seem right to me. It didn't seem true that God only wanted to be part of my life on Sundays but was detached from me during the week. I wasn't buying it.

So I decided to do some research, and I found that God has mandated us to *think, innovate,* and *create.* In the following chapters, I will share with you the discoveries I've made and a bit about my business journey. I hope these insights encourage you and help you move along the path God has called you to walk—especially if that path leads you into the realm of the marketplace. These insights will show you the purpose of enterprise, the vitality of vision, and how to ensure business success through environmental cultivation with pinpointed strategies that fit your business model and ultimately maximize your positive influence and impact.

—April Ripley

ACKNOWLEDGMENTS

To my Creator, who fashioned me with innate potential and capacity to think, innovate, and create. You created me on purpose, with purpose, and for purpose. Without Your words, there would be no truth.

To my family, who has been a strong support in my continuing discovery and the journey into the fulfillment of my purpose.

To all of my friends and colleagues who have walked with me along this purpose-filled journey, thank you.

To my mentors who see the gifts within and give sage insight to assist in their release.

To those whose tireless efforts went into the editing, designing, and publishing of this work, words cannot express my eternal gratitude.

To the readers of this work, know that you were created to Be Exceptional™ from the inside out.

Chapter 1

THE PURPOSE OF CREATION

Only the creator knows the purpose of a creation. —Dr. Myles Munroe

I decided to start my research by looking up the definition of *business*.

Business: noun—a person's regular occupation, profession, or trade. The practice of making one's living by engaging in commerce.[1]

So, business is the practice of a person's regular occupation that encompasses making one's living by engaging in commerce. But where did business begin? *Why* did business begin?

---

1. *Lexico*, s.v. "business," accessed June 13, 2020, *https://www.lexico.com/en/definition/business*.

I needed to find out more. And like all wise persons do, I started at the beginning. There had to be some clue in the Bible.

I went to Genesis 1:1. It said that in the beginning God prepared, formed, fashioned, and created the heavens. Wait! That seemed a lot like a working business to me. Isn't that what we do in business—prepare, form, fashion, and create things? I went to a Hebrew translation of this verse: "In the beginning God, Elohim, created, by forming from nothing, the heavens and the earth."

Business involves creating something from nothing but also creating something from something. That "something" in business is the discovery of a need. The need is created from the lack of something, or void, to meet that need. Business is the discovery of that lack and a determination to fill it.

When we look at God as the ultimate entrepreneur, we see that He created something from nothing. And from that creation, He created something else: mankind. Genesis 1:26–27 (AMP) says:

Then God said, "Let Us (Father, Son, Holy Spirit) make man in Our image, according to Our likeness [not physical, but a spiritual personality and moral likeness]; and let them have complete authority over the fish of the sea, the birds of the air, the cattle, and over the entire earth, and over everything that creeps and crawls on the earth." So, God created man in His own image, in

the image and likeness of God He created him; male and
female He created them.

In verse 27, two Hebrew words are used to describe the creation of man. The first is *bara*, which means "to create from nothing." The second is *as a*, which means "to form from something already created." This means that God used what He'd already made—the dust of the ground—and from it, He made man.

I was beginning to see some light at the end of the tunnel. In the act of creation, God created something from nothing, which is what we do in business. But why did He do it? Was there a purpose to creation? And was that purpose connected to what we do in business too?

CREATING FOR A PURPOSE

Creation is "the action or process of bringing something into existence; the bringing into existence of the universe, especially when regarded as an act of God; the action or process of investing someone with a new rank or title."[2] We see that creation is the result of a creator. Creation begins in the mind; it's a by-product of vision. This means that creation is intentional, purposed, pragmatic, and potent. A created thing has the capacity to fulfill the intention for which it was created.

---

2. Lexico, s.v. "creation," accessed June 13, 2020, *https://www.lexico.com/en/definition/creation*.

In Genesis 2:15 (AMP), we can clearly see God's purpose for man:

So the LORD God took the man [He had made] and settled him in the Garden of Eden to cultivate and keep it.

We also hear about this purpose in Genesis 1:28 (AMP):

And God blessed them [granting them certain authority] and said to them, "Be fruitful, multiply, and fill the earth, and subjugate it [putting it under your power]; and rule over (dominate) the fish of the sea, the birds of the air, and every living thing that moves upon the earth."

Here we see the purpose God had for man and His vision for a colony of heaven on earth through humanity. What God envisioned, we see displayed as vision. God had a purpose and then saw a void that would hinder the fulfillment of that purpose, so He cultivated an environment that would allow His purpose to work. Genesis 1 details the work God did in the heavens, earth, and sea to ensure that the purpose of mankind would be able to function properly.

Creation shows us the power of purpose. It is purpose—the why—that dictates the direction of the entire business. In God's act of creation, we see parallels of enterprise, which starts with exerted human effort of thought, creativity, and work—from concept to plan to implementation.

Purpose is the reason for the creation or existence of something; it involves intention. The purpose of creation is known by its creator. When you ask someone about the purpose or vision for your own business, they will not know. It's *your* vision! What others will recognize is your passion and conviction. The key is to be sure of your purpose for starting a business. What is it you want to do? Why do you want to do it? Discovering the purpose of your business will be the foundation upon which the mission stands. Depending on what your business is and in what industry you work, you will operate it in unique ways.

When I created The Premiere Image, Inc., I did so with the purpose of equipping persons with soft skills that would promote their success in personal and professional situations. As the persons and organizations I consulted began to grow in diversity and reach, I found myself traveling the world and influencing and impacting more persons that I had initially imagined. Although we are incorporating different methods to enlarge our reach, our original purpose has not changed.

Creation was a well-thought-out plan. God saw the future and recognized the importance of the present to foster the end result He wanted. Business owners must also look to where they want to go and initiate the appropriate strategies to get there. Given where we are today, with accelerated computing power, artificial intelligence, robotics, and automation, we must ensure that our businesses remain agile and collaborative. We live in the age of collaboration. This collaboration exists not only between mankind and machines, but also between humans and humans.

According to a report by H. James Wilson and Paul R. Daughtery titled "Collaborative Intelligence," published in *Harvard Business Review* in August 2018, businesses must employ five essential business processes in order to reach their desired results: flexibility, speed, scale, decision making, and personalization. We see these same processes inherent throughout creation. We see a King who created more kings and also created the environment in which they could perform the purpose for which they were created.

THE ROLE OF HIERARCHY

Let's take a look next at the detail of God's creation—hierarchy—and what this can tell us about how God does business.

In creation, we see the foundation of hierarchy. Hierarchy is not intended to suffocate but to inspire and aspire—to cover and protect. Hierarchy gives the protocols within which things can function in proper order and safety. It is a system or organization in which people or groups are ranked, one above the other, according to status or authority, and protocol is the accepted or established code of procedure or behavior in any group, organization, or situation. The detail of

God in creation set the hierarchy and established the protocol of how God did business and how we should do business.

So, creation started with envisioned purpose in the mind of God. We've already seen that God wanted a colony of heaven on earth to be managed by mankind (Genesis 2:15). In business, this would be like a franchise of the parent company. The parent company (in this case, God) gives the franchisee (which is us) the right to operate the business under the protection and auspices of the parent company. On a larger scale, God's idea for Kingdom colonization was like a multinational company whose offices and/or factories operate in different countries (this would be all the nations of the world) with a centralized head office (heaven) that coordinates global management. This is the hierarchy.

Then comes the protocol. God sets the expectations for how things are to function, which we already saw in Genesis 1:28 (AMP):

"Be fruitful, multiply, and fill the earth, and subjugate it [putting it under your power]; and rule over (dominate) the fish of the sea, the birds of the air, and every living thing that moves upon the earth."

Protocol provides confidence in the operation and working of any enterprise. In business today, we see this through human resource departments, which are the entities that administer and enforce the policies and procedures, meaning the protocols and hierarchy, of the companies they serve.

Another example is the instructions that are included with products. These pamphlets give insight into the order of the product: how to turn it on and off, how to operate it safely, and how to maximize the benefit of the product. Following the prescribed protocol is vital to its functions.

We'll explore this idea of protocol as God set it up in more detail in the next chapter.

CHOOSING A LOCATION

Creation also shows us the importance of real estate, or location, in business. God began to cultivate the environment and atmosphere for His business to thrive. The first thing the Word tells us is that the earth was "formless and void" (Genesis 1:2, AMP). There was no structure and thus no productivity of function. But God envisioned something different and began to cultivate the location necessary for the sustainability and growth of His creation. How did He bring it about? He used the most valuable real estate available: intellectual property. From the idea of His creation, He secured and developed real estate (land and property), starting with the sky and spreading to the earth and to the sea.

The same is true in our business today. Once we have our vision, we too must secure the property from where the business will operate. This may be a physical location or a virtual location. We must have vision and then find the location—the real estate—that allows us to make the vision a reality.

One's choice in this matter is no small thing. Can you imagine someone selling ice to people living in the Arctic? Of course not. They already have the natural resources to keep things cold and preserve them; ice is all around them. However, in a warm climate, where keeping things cold is an arduous task, the selling of ice would be more profitable. Location is key.

Amazon is another example of the importance of real estate. Jeff Bezos knew that having thousands of brick-and-mortar stores would be costly, so what did he do? He found another type of real estate: the internet. He found people who already had products and created a platform (a central online location) where those people could sell their products and everyone could purchase what they needed.

You may not think Jeff Bezos created anything; after all, he used other people's products, right? But that's exactly the point. He created a system that enabled what already existed to be formed into something new: a global marketplace. Sometimes in business, we look for new things to create. Other times it's more profitable and rewarding to take what's already there and enhance it for further impact.

Where you are right now? What do you see around you? Do you see a swamp that could become the next Atlantis? What you allow your mind to envision is what you will see become reality.

PLANNING FOR CHANGE

God created a structure before breathing life into man—just like, before receiving funding for a business, you must develop a business plan. You need an outline, a defined structure. Only after the structure is organized can the life of the business begin.

As marketplace people, we must realize that our world is ever changing. Research by the World Economic Forum concluded in 2016 that "five years from now, over one-third of skills (35%) that are considered important in today's workforce will have changed."[3]

Furthermore, a professor at Oklahoma State University addressed, in 2018, the shift in educational systems and learning methods:

Online learning has put as many as half the colleges and universities in the U.S. at risk of shutting down in the next couple decades as remote students get comparable educations over the internet—without living on campus or taking classes in person. Unless universities move

---

3. Alex Gray, "The 10 Skills You Need to Thrive in the Fourth Industrial Revolution," January 19, 2016, World Economic Forum, *https://www.weforum.org/agenda/2016/01/the-10-skills-you-need-to-thrive-in-the-fourth-industrial-revolution/.*

quickly to transform themselves into educational institutions for a technology-assisted future, they risk becoming obsolete.[4]

Research has additionally concluded that by the time college students reach their senior year, almost half of the information they learned in university will have become obsolete.

How does one not only survive but thrive in such an environment? We must be students, continually learning. What are the emerging trends? Where is the world moving? What are the needs of humanity? As the population grows, what are the needs among different generations?

This comes down to planning. Planning is crucial for every human, whether you own a business or work for a company—and even just for you as your own person. Why? Because time and chance happen to us all (Ecclesiastes 9:11). Time progresses for everyone, and chance is the unknown.

Change is the constant of time and chance. Everything living changes, by nature and design. Some may have the attitude that "Whatever is to be, will be, so why would I plan anything, not knowing what will be?" True. However, it is in that very statement of not knowing that you should plan, because you don't know.

---

4. Subhash Kak, "Universities Must Prepare for a Technology-Enabled Future," January 9, 2018, *The Conversation, https:// theconversation.com/universities-must-prepare-for-a-technology-enabled-future-89354?xid=PS_smithsonian.*

We cannot ignore change. Change is inevitable. A wise person plans for the future, because it will come.

Risk management in business identifies, evaluates, and prioritizes risks and then allocates specified resources to minimize and control the probability of impact, should change or unforeseen events arise. If you are not able to do this yourself, seek the advice of a risk management specialist. Remember that wisdom is found in counsel. Also remember this: Thinking promulgates change. Innovation provokes change. Creation propels change.

WE'RE HERE TO SOLVE PROBLEMS

The key to business success is to solve a problem—and God was the first problem solver. He saw a dark void, which means He recognized a problem. Then He began to fill that void. He solved the problem.

In business, we identify problems through research. Then we must acknowledge the problem and find out how it came to be. What are its effects? Remember, you cannot solve a problem on the same level on which that problem was created, but you must understand the level on which it came to be in order to find solutions. This is what an entrepreneur does. Whether you own your business or work for someone else, you are ultimately a problem solver.

In today's marketplace, we are told to stand up, speak out, and stand out. We celebrate and encourage the search for the uncommon, the new, and the disruptive. I am often asked, "How do I make more money? How do I get a promotion?" My answer is, "Find a problem, and solve it."

Problem-finding appears to be the antithesis of our society today, though. We try our best to avoid problems. We hear sayings like "Don't ruffle any feathers" or "Don't rock the boat" or "Hear no evil, speak no evil, see no evil." We like our comfort zones.

However, no one in history is remembered for staying in his or her comfort zone. The ones we remember are those who gave up their comfort to make impact and change in their communities and the world. Business is not comfortable. It is not remaining in a stagnant mindset.

Remember Blockbuster? It was a brick-and-mortar powerhouse video rental company that appeared impregnable. And then came along this little startup, Netflix, that decided to offer the convenience of movie rentals delivered directly to the mailboxes of its customers.

Where are Blockbuster and Netflix now? Blockbuster no longer exists because it did not want to change with the market's demand for at-home convenience. People wanted to rent a video without having to go into a physical store to get it, especially when—and this was the worst—there was a chance the video would already have been rented out.

Netflix, on the other hand, founded in 1997 by Reed Hastings and Marc Randolph, saw the demand of people wanting to watch a movie in their home without ever having to leave their home to get it, coupled with the rise of in-home internet use. It now has more than 182 million paid subscriptions worldwide, including 69 million in the United States,[5] and also produces its own content (Wikipedia).

How many people over the age of 25 remember Blockbuster? In contrast, how many people know about Netflix?

GOD, THE FIRST ENTREPRENEUR

Wow! It was there all this time, in the Scripture. God Himself had created it.

I find it interesting that God chose to have His Son born into a family of entrepreneurs in the business of carpentry (Matthew 13:55; Mark 6:3). From age two until age 12, Jesus was working in the home and business of a carpenter. Then, from age 12 until age 30, we have no information to indicate He did anything else. For all we know, He was still working in the family business, as was the custom. Jesus was a builder,

---

5. Wikipedia, s.v. "Netflix," accessed June 14, 2020, *https://en.wikipedia.org/wiki/Netflix.*

a craftsman; surely those skills and perspectives also align with what He did in ministry, both throughout the Gospels and to this day.

Jesus worked in the home and business of his earthly father, Joseph. He would have learned types of wood, design and craftsmanship, along with other skills necessary for conducting a successful business, such as management, accounting, and resource allocation.

It is no accident that Jesus was the earthly son of a father whose job was to build things for the comfort and practical use of the livelihood of humanity. This is what Jesus' ministry was about: building people and leaving a structure called the *ekklesia* in place, which would aid in the betterment of life through a relationship with God.

God created everything with purpose and on purpose. Creation was the first entrepreneurial act in history. God created in immense detail and made a way for His creation to be managed and perpetuated, involving mankind in this process. Through creation, we see a beautiful blueprint for business—an order, intentionality, and detail that we're still only beginning to uncover.

Chapter 2

THE FIVE COMMANDS OF CREATION

You can't use up creativity. The more you use the more you have. —Maya Angelou

We see that God created the structure and environment for His business, extending His influence of heaven to earth. Then He had to manage the earth's resources. How would He choose to do this?

Let's look again at Genesis 1:28 (AMP):

And God blessed them [granting them certain authority] and said to them, "Be fruitful, multiply, and fill the earth, and subjugate it [putting it under your power]; and rule over (dominate) the fish of the sea, the birds of the air, and every living thing that moves upon the earth."

Scripture says God blessed them and gave them five commands. Notice that God first gave them the *ability* to do and then *commanded* them to do. God will never demand of us what He has not given us the ability to do. It stands to reason that if He commands us to do something, He has already placed the ability—and resources—within our grasp.

Now let's look at each of the five commands He gave.

1. THE COMMAND TO BE FRUITFUL

First, God commanded mankind to be fruitful. This doesn't simply mean that He wanted them to have a lot of babies. In order to be fruitful, you must be seedful. Being seedful means that within every individual is the potential to grow something, which itself will have more potential to grow, and so on and so on. Before fruit grows, it is hidden in the seed; once the fruit reaches maturity, the seed is hidden in the fruit. Everything created has within itself the seed to reproduce. This is what science calls the "reproduction cycle"—and all living things have it.

As a business, what have you produced that will allow you to bring more fruit—more seed? For example, if you bake cookies for family gatherings, can those same cookies be made and sold to others, to stores, or even online? Do you have anything already in you that can produce more fruit?

I recall my friend Tracye Carter, founder of Tracye's Culinary Creations and her world-famous Tracye's Chicken Salad Dressing. Tracye was always one to host dinner parties and insist on preparing everything. The dinner presentations were elegant, but the food was starlit. The dish that became her claim to future fame was her chicken salad.

Tracye's consistency in her product and service at dinners and get-togethers led to large catering contracts. I even had her cater my first book launch! She and I met one night for dinner to talk further about the far-reaching potential of her chicken salad. After our conversation, additional business research and counsel, and a leap of faith, her product is now available in all of the Whole Foods Markets in the Southeast.

Tracye started her business with a seed of a skill—culinary skill. She continued to develop it by learning more about food—how to prepare it on a larger scale, how to market it, and more. Was it an easy process? No. Did it cost something to make it happen? Yes, it cost time, energy, some no's, and even financial investments. However, if you ask Tracye today if it was all worth it, she would tell you yes.

What Tracye did was based on a conviction in her heart. She was determined to see her vision come to pass. I celebrate her for her courage and tenacity. She encountered a few bumps in the road on the way to re-alizing her vision. But not only has she grown her busi-ness, she has also met incredible people and support-ers along the way. And I know more is in store for her!

What seed do you have? What are you doing to make that seed grow? In order for a seed to grow, it needs the proper environment—soil, water, and sun. Ensuring that your skill develops means cultivating the things you need to ensure its growth.

This means that you will need to invest in yourself. You may have to take classes, read books, and attend seminars or conferences to learn something new. Growing anything takes equity—sweat equity first, and then financial equity. You also have to watch out for the predators that think your seed is tasty, like the naysayers, the haters, or even the competitors. And be careful of those who are close to you who, with all good intentions, will seek to "protect you" from doing some-thing "that may fail" but who can't see the same vision for your future that you see.

The associations and people you choose to surround yourself with are factors in your reaching your desired destination. You have to be discerning, and remem-ber that in the multitude of counsel, there is safety. Having an understanding of the factors that weigh in on your business development are vital. This is where a business plan is critical. A business plan helps you to look through the many lenses that make a business successful. But do not forget that it starts with you, the visionary. And even with all the counsel you receive, you must make the final decision to move forward or retreat.

Lastly, don't forget your character. Your character is a composite of your values, beliefs, and attitude. Even if you plant the seed in the right soil and water it, the catalyst for its growth is the sun. When the right attitude and values, like humility and integrity, mix together, it causes the stem to grow.

Remain faithful and committed to your seed. Nurture it properly, and you will see it grow into more than what it was originally. An apple is the fruit that grew from a tree that grew from a seed. It all begins as a seed.

2. THE COMMAND TO MULTIPLY

The second command is to multiply, which implies we are to reproduce in mass quantity. Being seedful allows for multiplication. How does this translate into business terms? Multiplication is increase. This multiplication requires a system to ensure that the reproductive cycle sustains itself so that what we produce is able to increase and multiply exponentially.

Let me give you an example of this. In the early 1900s, African-American businesswoman and philanthropist Madame C. J. Walker (also known as Sarah Breedlove) sold her products door-to-door, teaching women how to style their hair. Later, Madame Walker began a mail-order operation, opened a beauty parlor, and established Lelia College of Beauty Culture to train "hair culturists." This ultimately led to a national network of licensed sales agents, who each earned a healthy commission. Madame Walker took one service—hair care—and multiplied the avenues of distribution for her products. She transitioned from door-to-door sales to direct sales to training and education. Later on, she became a philanthropist and social entrepreneur, equipping and empowering women of color with skills and access to resources.[6]

Multiplication is also seen in business franchises. McDonald's is an example of this. What appeared to be good, quickly prepared burgers morphed into a globally recognized company, leveraging real estate ownership through the vehicle of franchise.

Multiplication can be a collaborative effort, a strategic partnership, or a joint venture. It allows for diversification and value augmentation. It aligns with the African proverb that says, "If you want to go fast, go alone, but if you want to go far, go together."

---

6. Wikipedia, s.v. "Madam C. J. Walker," accessed June 14, 2020, *https://en.wikipedia.org/wiki/Madam_C._J._Walker.*

3. THE COMMAND TO REPLENISH

God next commands mankind to replenish. This is because as production happens and multiplication is ensured, there may still be areas that lack abundance. These would need to be replenished. Duplication and distribution would be key. Mankind would have to figure out how to distribute what God had given them.

We look at Jesus and see that for three years, He created a system of fruitfulness, multiplication, and replenishment in twelve men. Today, His system is still working—still making disciples. Distribution is key, because it allows the product or service to reach beyond local areas and go global. This is the part of business that allows you to make money while you sleep.

When we look at replenishing, we also need to look at the element of scale. Scalability means that a business experiences competitive advantage as it grows, in a capable and cost-effective manner.

The Coca-Cola Company recognized the necessity of replenishing. It was originally marketed and intended as a patent medicine in the late nineteenth century by John Stith Pemberton and was bought out by businessman Asa Griggs Candler, whose marketing tactics led to its dominance of the global soft-drink market.[7]

---

7. Wikipedia, s.v. "The Coca-Cola Company," accessed June 14, 2020, *https://en.wikipedia.org/wiki/Coca-Cola*.

The key to the ability to replenish the product was using global licensed bottlers. The Coca-Cola Company wisely leveraged partnership to expand. It catered to its strength—producing carbonated beverages—and allowed for another company's strength—bottling—to become a part of the aggregate, which has led it to become the world's leading supplier of sparkling and still beverages.[8]

4. THE COMMAND TO SUBDUE

God also commanded mankind to subdue. For us in business, this means we begin to control the markets. We develop something that pays over and over.

This command is where your gifting becomes your source of business authority. Proverbs 18:16 (AMP) says, "A man's gift [given in love or courtesy] makes room for him and brings him before great men."

In the original ancient Hebrew text, the word *subdue* is *kabash* (כָּבַשׁ), which is commonly translated as "to subdue" or "bring into bondage." Merriam-Webster defines subdue as a transitive verb with four meanings:[9]
1. to conquer and bring into subjection: vanquish
2. to bring under control especially by an exertion of the will: curb

---

8. QTC Recruitment, "Top 10 World's Largest Food and Beverage Companies in 2017," accessed June 14, 2020, *https://qtcrecruitment.com/top-10-worlds-largest-food-beverage-companies-2017.*
9. *https://www.merriam-webster.com/dictionary/subdue*

3. to bring (land) under cultivation

4. to reduce the intensity or degree of: tone down

From the above definitions, we can see that subduing in business means vanquishing a need in humanity through the cultivation of allocated resources. The quagmire we see not only determines the need of resources we will utilize, but also to what extent we will do so. What is our responsibility to the earth and our fellow humans?

We must address this predicament of nature and humanity from the biblical interpretation of environment and societal progress. In 1986, the Christian Declaration on Nature, which was part of the multi-denominational Assisi Declarations based upon the writings of St. Francis Assisi, declared this:

> *Most certainly, then, because of the responsibilities which flow from his dual citizenship, man's dominion cannot be understood as license to abuse, spoil, squander or destroy what God has made to manifest his glory. That dominion cannot be anything other than a stewardship in symbiosis with all creatures.*[10]

In his recent encyclical letter, *Laudato Sí*, Pope Francis responded to the charge that Genesis grants humans the right to exploit the natural world without limits:

---

10. Alliance of Religions and Conservation, "The Assisi Declarations: Messages on Humanity and Nature from Buddhism, Christianity, Hinduism, Islam, and Judaism," September 29, 1986, *http://www.arcworld.org/downloads/THE%20ASSISI%20DECLARATIONS.pdf.*

Although it is true that we Christians have at times incorrectly interpreted the Scriptures, nowadays we must forcefully reject the notion that our being created in God's image and given dominion over the earth justifies absolute domination over other creatures. The biblical texts are to be read in their context, with an appropriate hermeneutic, recognizing that they tell us to "till and keep" the garden of the world (cf. Gen 2:15). "Tilling" refers to cultivating, ploughing or working, while "keeping" means caring, protecting, overseeing and preserving. This implies a relationship of mutual responsibility between human beings and nature.[11]

All of the above arguments prove mankind's responsibility and liability for the natural environment, as given by the command to "work it and take care of it" (Genesis 2:15, NIV). *Work* and *care* convey the message that this is an active and consistent effort. It begins with mental processing. How you view a thing determines your perspective of the thing.

In order to meet a need, businesses must first look at the situation from the view of the stakeholders. Taking this view is only the beginning in project management protocol. Stakeholders are not just equity investors; they are all parties and entities that are a part of the

---

11. Pope Francis, "Encyclical Letter *Laudato Sí* of the Holy Father Francis on Care for Our Common Home," May 24, 2015, http://www.vatican.va/content/francesco/en/encyclicals/documents/papa-francesco_20150524_enciclica-laudato-si.html.

process, from concept to production, and this includes the results that come at the conclusion.

Let's look at this principle by examining a clothing manufacturing business. A partial list of the stakeholders would include equity investors, board members, employees, customers, families of employees, families of customers, the community where the building is located, the environment surrounding the building, suppliers, vendors, and so on and so forth.

In an article for *Entrepreneur*, Hostt co-founder Peter Daisyme writes, "It's one thing to come up with a great idea and execute on it; it's another to anticipate the next market need and shift to meet it while expanding internal processes and capabilities."[12] This means, again, consideration must be taken of scale and what is needed to actualize growth.

For some businesses, this could mean employing a retrenchment strategy to reduce operations and cut back on expenses. Subduing also entails anticipating future needs for products or services. Those who are able to deftly do this find themselves still in business. Those who cannot become like Sears, Toys"R"Us, and Blockbuster or find themselves losing market share, like Blackberry or Motorola. Recalibration and restructuring are vital components to repositioning businesses for success.

---

12. Peter Daisyme, "Most CEOs Miss These 3 Things When Scaling Their Businesses," August 31, 2018, https://www.entrepreneur.com/article/318750.

5. THE COMMAND TO DOMINATE

The next key word in Genesis 1:28 is *dominion*. In the original ancient Hebrew text, this word is *radah* (רדה), meaning "to rule over" or "dominate."

This doesn't mean that we dominate people but rather the resources in, above, and surrounding the earth. This is why God told Adam what was beneath him in the ground and walked Adam around the garden to show him what was there. This is even why God had Adam name the animals. God wanted Adam to know and recognize all the resources He was entrusting to him.

I find it interesting that God told Adam in Genesis 2 what was beneath him. I believe God wanted Adam to recognize the things he couldn't see at that point in time but would come to see, as man developed the ability to dig into the earth. One day, people would be able to harness all the minerals and resources in the earth to create all kinds of things—tools, clothing, chairs, sofas, cars, computers, cell phones, and so on.

This requires a kind of faith. The Bible tells us that faith is the substance of things we hope for and the evidence of what we can't see. Adam couldn't see what was beneath him, yet God's word to him was evidence of its existence. Only by having faith in God could mankind go on to dominate the earth and utilize its resources in full.

When you think of domination in an industry, you think of a company that has captured its industry through innovation, service, speed, agility, and user satisfaction.

For instance, have you ever said, "I'll Google that"? Google is a search engine platform; however, it has so dominated the search engine space that its name has become a verb synonymous with the actual action of searching anything online.

What about Xerox? The Xerox Corporation manufactures copier machines. Again, its name has become synonymous with the action in many conversations. Saying, "Could you Xerox that document?" is the same as saying, "Could you copy that document?"

Shall we venture into the ride-hailing space of Uber? "I'm Ubering there," again, has become synonymous with the ride-sharing action.

Globally, Microsoft has dominated computers with its operating system. Whether you utilize a personal computer or MacBook, Microsoft's suite of software programs, from Word to Excel to PowerPoint and more, has compatible versions. These are not only recognized but also utilized the world over.

How does a company dominate its industry? Diversifying its good or services, cutting consumer costs, providing exceptional service, and including competitive advantages name a few strategies.

Industry domination is not haphazard. It is done with intentionality and clear goals.

ENHANCE YOUR GIFTS

Your seed is your gift, and your seed is within you. What is within you? An idea? A product? A service? This is connected to your purpose. What you do to grow and develop it is called *skill*.

This seed, or gift, is often called a *propensity*. Propensity comes from the Latin *propensus*, meaning "inclined," so it is a natural tendency or inclination to behave in a certain way. Your purpose, then, is tied to what you have a natural inclination and ability to do. The discovery of your gift allows you to then develop and hone the skills necessary to promulgate your gift.

Here's what this can look like as applied to my own vantage point. From the time I was young, I was always talking to people—in elevators, in malls, on the playground, wherever. My parents told me not all people had good intentions and that talking to strangers may not always be wise, especially if my parents weren't around. But I liked talking to people. Today I have traveled around the world speaking and training, educating, and empowering people to be their best selves—to discover and release the greatness that lies within them. I believe my "never meeting a stranger gift" has found its purpose.

I believe that discovering my gift of congeniality has led me into the sphere of diplomacy. The noun *congeniality* is closely related to the word *geniality*, which means "friendliness." Congeniality can be defined the same way, but the Latin prefix *con*, or "with," adds a sense of connection to other people. I started attending seminars that promoted personal development, read books on understanding human interactions, trained at a school where diplomats are sent to train, and eventually became a part of an international organization made up of more than 80 nations, which eventually led me to working with an NGO in special economic consultative status with the United Nations, which is comprised of 193 nations. Although each step in my journey was not the same, the path led down the same road—connecting people to people—which began by "never meeting strangers" at a young age.

Remember that every human is born with innate gifts. Discover your gift, and hone the skills necessary to enhance that gift. You enhance your gift by investing in skills that will polish it. And when your gift is polished, it can garner the attention of influential persons, allowing you to eventually become a person of that same circle.

A gift is an inherent ability to fulfill a need. Gifts are not earned; they are just simply a part of you. A bird flies because flight is innate in it. Fish swim because it is innate in them to do so. What is innate in man? The ability to think, innovate, and create.

I have been blessed to travel the world. I've seen some wealthy places, and I've seen some very poor places. I would reason that both the shelters built in the wealthy places and those constructed in the poor places were resourceful and innovative. I have seen blankets placed as canopies over heads and boxes laid end-to-end on the ground. I am not saying this is ideal; I am saying it shows the creative and resourceful nature innate in man.

Gifts are often discovered, while skills are learned, developed, enhanced, and refined. Skills most often complement one's gifts. Parents and guardians see this while they are raising children. They'll see proclivities and aptitudes for certain things and say to themselves, "How do they know to do that?"

One example of this is my little "sister," Victoria. Whenever she finishes playing with a toy, she puts it back where she got it. When she finishes using a dish, she begins to wash and dry it. She even sweeps the floor! Even as a young girl of six years old, the gift of organization and order was evident in Miss Victoria. As she grows older, she will have opportunity to develop her skill in school, in work, and in whatever she decides to do. Her gifts will be like a thread woven throughout the tapestry of her life.

Chapter 3

THE FOUR *Rs* OF CREATION

Details matter, and so does an eagle's point of view.
—Rosangel Perez

So, God created the perfect atmosphere, Eden, for mankind to fulfill all of the commands He gave—to be fruitful, to multiply, to replenish, to subdue, and to dominate. This atmosphere is where Adam walked and talked with his Creator, communing with Him and creating an intimacy of spirit and soul. But you may wonder, *Why would God go through all of the preparation of creation to cultivate an organized and sustaining environment? After six days, everything was already made and working. What did He want man to do?*

God created an ordered and balanced environment for man to flourish—a garden. And from that garden, He created everything that would grow, sustain, and progress mankind. The answer to the purpose of man's creation is found in Genesis 2:5 (NIV):

Now no shrub had yet appeared on the earth and no plant had yet sprung up, for the LORD God had not sent rain on the earth and there was no one to work the ground.

God had not yet allowed what would promulgate his fivefold command because He had not yet instructed Adam. Adam needed to understand the plants and animals. He needed to have this knowledge or chaos would ensue.

Genesis 2:6 (NIV) says, "But streams came up from the earth and watered the whole surface of the ground." God allowed the ground to be wet to prepare for man, but God did not allow the growth of plants and shrubs until after He created man. If we jump ahead to verse 15 (NIV), we find the moment where man enters the scene: "The LORD God took the man and put him in the Garden of Eden to work it and take care of it."

Work was what God did, and work is what God created man to do. God began telling Adam what was available to him as resources for his mission. We see these resources a few verses earlier, in Genesis 2:9–17 (NIV). Let's take a look:

The LORD God made all kinds of trees grow out of the ground—trees that were pleasing to the eye and good

*for food. In the middle of the garden were the tree of life
and the tree of the knowledge of good and evil.*

*A river watering the garden flowed from Eden; from there it
was separated into four headwaters. The name of the first
is the Pishon; it winds through the entire land of Havilah,
where there is gold. (The gold of that land is good; aromatic
resin and onyx are also there.) The name of the second river
is the Gihon; it winds through the entire land of Cush. The
name of the third river is the Tigris; it runs along the east
side of Ashur. And the fourth river is the Euphrates.*

*The LORD God took the man and put him in the Garden
of Eden to work it and take care of it. And the LORD God
commanded the man, "You are free to eat from any tree
in the garden; but you must not eat from the tree of the
knowledge of good and evil, for when you eat from it you
will certainly die."*

Many of the resources God shared with Adam flowed
near and around him. This emphasizes that water is
essential not only to life but in the development and
sustenance of it—physically, socially, and economical-
ly. Even spiritually, water is necessary; Jesus said He
is the Living Water, and Psalm 1 describes believers as
those planted by rivers of living water.

God told Adam what was above ground and beneath
the ground. In doing so, God also gave Adam four *R*s
that we'll now explore. These principles apply to us
as well, as we steward, lead, and manage our resources today.

RESOURCES

God gave Adam resources—trees, fruit, water, and land, as well as the knowledge of things that lay beneath him, soon to be discovered. Ultimately, Adam was to comprehend the uses of all these resources, apply his knowledge, and begin to create.

There are several definitions of resources, all which describe what mankind was given:[13]

- a stock or supply of money, materials, staff, and other assets that can be drawn on by a person or organization in order to function effectively
- a country's collective means of supporting itself or becoming wealthier, as represented by its reserves of minerals, land, and other natural assets
- an action or strategy which may be adopted in adverse circumstances
- one's personal attributes and capabilities regarded as able to help or sustain one in adverse circumstances
- the ability to find quick and clever ways to overcome difficulties

The resources given to humanity were both tangible and intangible. It is the intangible (thoughts, ideas, and concepts) that allow for the creativity and innovation of the tangible (people and physical things).

---

13. Lexico, s.v. "resource," accessed June 14, 2020, *https://www.lexico.com/en/definition/resource.*

REAL ESTATE

Adam also received property. The first kind of property was the garden itself, of course. But God gave Adam another property besides the garden. This second kind of property was more expansive than Hong Kong, London, and New York today. It was the kind of property that thinks of, innovates, and creates all other resources. It was intellectual property.

The intellect is the faculty of reasoning and understanding objectively, especially with regard to abstract matters. Therefore, intellectual property, also known as IP, is the creation of the mind.

Intellectual property includes inventions, literary and artistic works, designs, and symbols, names, and images used in commerce. This is what God breathed into man when he became a living being. This is the power of vision and purpose. It begins in the mind.

The mind is able to see things without tangibly taking them in through sight. It sees through faith and hope. Intellectual property unlocks for us the capability to allocate and manage resources, to find synergy and opportunities, and to form ideas and collaborate.

These are what God did in creation, and we have that capability too because He gave us the same *modus operandi*. Even the four types of IP—trade secrets, trademarks, copyrights, and patents—outline the various areas of creativity and idea formulation.

Everyone and everything were created on purpose for a purpose. To determine the purpose of a thing, you must go to the one who created it. Intellect births creativity, and creativity molds, shapes, and designs. How does one determine his or her purpose? By going to the creator, the source of the design. Then one discovers the problem he was created to solve. Everything created solves a problem. What are the problems around you? Once you figure that out, your mind begins to formulate solutions to fix, solve, or ease the problems you see.

Sometimes we think we have to come up with the next big thing. But often innovation comes by tweaking what already exists. Think about the shoe industry. Comfortable, affordable shoes have been around for decades. Yet when TOMS came along, the founders tied their profits to a social cause. Customers knew that when they purchased a pair of TOMS, they were also paying for a pair to be sent to a child that didn't own shoes through the company's "buy one, give one" program.

This disrupted the profit-making industry because it tied social impact and the well-being of others to business profits. Today we call this social enterprise, or corporate social responsibility. Corporations can no longer just pillage for profit; there has to be accountability.

Accountability has always been tied to ability. My mentor, Dr. Myles Munroe, often said, "Do not follow anyone who does not want to be account-able." Even in our government, the three branches provide checks and balances; each is accountable to the other to operate in accordance with the law. Accountability fosters integrity, creativity, loyalty, discipline, and character.

The first thing man was to do was protect the environment. This is why the Creator showed Adam all of the things around him. When man abuses his environment, he abuses himself. The environment is critical to man's function and to the functions of all other life. When the balance is disturbed, as we are seeing today, glaciers melt and unprecedented levels of natural disasters occur. One wonders if these are "natural" disasters or, in fact, man-made. We must be careful in our desire to create and innovate that we do not abuse our environment—this may destroy us, as well.

RELATIONSHIPS

In order for man to fully comprehend and apply what he knew, to the betterment of man and community, God knew Adam would need knowledge and insight beyond his own. I have learned that we reach up to learn, and we reach down to bring along. This is what creates the synergy of relationships.

Adam walked with God. Walking with wise people makes you wise. It's not just walking alongside a person that makes one wise. It's learning, (knowledge), understanding (comprehension) and application (wisdom) that leads to success in all areas of life.

Proverbs 4:7 says that wisdom, the ability to apply comprehended knowledge, is preeminent. From the Latin, this means that wisdom towers above all else. When Adam walked in relationship with God, he became like Him—wise and knowledgeable. Proverbs also says that "iron sharpens iron." A diamond cutter knows that you can only cut a diamond with another diamond. Relationships are meant to make us sharper, better, wiser.

Are you around people who sharpen you and cause you to think and act above the mediocre? Your associations construct your reputation. Who you spend time with reflects your character. Relationships are the bridges we walk across into our destiny. While Adam walked with God, his future was sure and sealed.

RESPONSIBILITY

The last "R" Adam received was responsibility. Adam was responsible to guard, govern, protect, and safeguard the garden. Adam was to cultivate—collect, manage, and maximize—the resources to bring about growth.

So, how do we define management? Management is the effective and efficient use of resources to produce added-value results. This simply means we bring about more than was originally there. This is the way the wealthy think. Poor people think about money. Rich people think about things. Wealthy people think about ideas. The wealthy know ideas bring money and other resources, so they begin with purpose and vision, just like God did. When you start in the proper order and wisdom dictates what should be preeminent, you will be successful.

Now, this isn't the same as waving a wand and seeing success at your door. Success and responsibility are still matters of hard work—intentional equity, investing the sweat and the finances and the time. Sometimes people won't see or support your vision. But responsibility leads to success.

From the beginning, we see that man was to manage resources. No matter how many jobs we automate, there will always be a need for us to take responsibility. The relational and logical thinking—the intellect that is predisposed to humans—will always be needed. This points us, once again, to our Creator.

The Creator did not create a world in which He would not be needed. No matter what industry or profession we examine, there is some part of it that was sourced by the Creator. Medicine? God made the plants. Education? God made the subjects we study. Science? God made atmospheres and matter. Sports? God made the materials to fashion balls and helmets.

Everything man has made derives from something God had already made. Even the air we breathe in and out—the air plants take and release into the atmosphere—God made it all. God inspired us with His breath, and only when God's breath leaves us do we expire. Concepts and theories that have long existed, created by God, are still being discovered by man today.

The details of creation are vast, and they point us both toward God and toward our God-given charge to steward them well. Let's take a closer look at the responsibility of stewardship and how it ties in to business enterprise.

Chapter 4

THE CALL TO STEWARDSHIP

Stewardship is the hallmark of life on earth.
—Sunday Adelaja

n the last chapter, we explored how God formed every single detail of creation. We see our utter dependence on Him and our responsibility to both multiply and steward the limited resources He's given us. This is a call to stewardship and leadership over what we have been given.

In his book *The Spirit of Leadership*, Dr. Myles Munroe defines leadership as the capacity to influence others through inspiration motivated by passion, generated by vision, produced by conviction, and ignited by purpose. This looks different to different people.

Richard Branson, for instance, has a very different style than Steve Jobs:

He contrasted his own leadership style—which is collaborative and democratic—to that of the late Steve Jobs (co-founder of Apple), who was known for his autocratic style. Despite their differences, both have experienced great success with their own philosophy and approach. There are no hard and fast rules about which leadership skills work the best; it is all about choosing a style that fits the organisation and optimizes the talent available.[14]

In Matthew 25:14–30 (NIV), we read a story about stewardship, which is management of another's resources. Let's take a look at it together:

Again, it will be like a man going on a journey, who called his servants and entrusted his wealth to them. To one he gave five bags of gold, to another two bags, and to another one bag, each according to his ability. Then he went on his journey. The man who had received five bags of gold went at once and put his money to work and gained five bags more. So also, the one with two bags of gold gained two more. But the man who had received one bag went off, dug a hole in the ground and hid his master's money.

After a long time, the master of those servants returned and settled accounts with them. The man who had

14. Robert Half, "Nine Leadership Skills from Sir Richard Branson," April 24, 2018, *https://www.roberthalf.ae/advice/people-management/9-leadership-skills-sir-richard-branson.*

received five bags of gold brought the other five. "Master," he said, "you entrusted me with five bags of gold. See, I have gained five more."

His master replied, "Well done, good and faithful servant! You have been faithful with a few things; I will put you in charge of many things. Come and share your master's happiness!"

The man with two bags of gold also came. "Master," he said, "you entrusted me with two bags of gold; see, I have gained two more."

His master replied, "Well done, good and faithful servant! You have been faithful with a few things; I will put you in charge of many things. Come and share your master's happiness!"

Then the man who had received one bag of gold came. "Master," he said, "I knew that you are a hard man, harvesting where you have not sown and gathering where you have not scattered seed. So I was afraid and went out and hid your gold in the ground. See, here is what belongs to you."

His master replied, "You wicked, lazy servant! So you knew that I harvest where I have not sown and gather where I have not scattered seed? Well then, you should have put my money on deposit with the bankers, so that when I returned I would have received it back with interest.

"So, take the bag of gold from him and give it to the one who has ten bags. For whoever has will be given more, *and they will have an abundance. Whoever does not have, even what they have will be taken from them. And throw that worthless servant outside, into the darkness, where there will be weeping and gnashing of teeth."*

In this parable, Jesus describes the Kingdom of heaven with the picture of a businessman going on a journey. He leaves managers, or stewards, entrusted with his resources. The businessman owns the resources—this is clear from the text. But each steward has been taught how to manage, and add value to, the resources. They are expected to do so. Otherwise the master would not leave the resources in their care.

THE CONSIDERATION OF CAPACITY

One of the key principles within this story is that stewardship is given based on the ability of each individual—his or her capacity to manage. We don't read much into the master's capacity or ability, but we can infer that he was sufficient in both because he was able to have managers working for him. The master was actively working the principles of management and enterprise.

We learn that the master was looking to return to find more than he'd left. He was looking for added value, which is profit. The entry-level steward had been given one talent; we can probably conclude, then, that each steward had started the management journey with one talent and had worked up to managing more.

This is encouraging to know because it means everyone comes to earth with something. We all have something to manage, and it's up to us to develop and add value to our unique resources. The entry-level servant had one talent; the second servant had started there, but now he had two talents; and the servant with five talents had grown significantly to get to the point of managing that many resources.

What could have been the factors that determined their trustworthiness to the master? Learning, hard work, diligence. Understanding and wisdom. Comprehension of business skills and strategies. Their observation of the master. The propensity to ask questions. Perhaps being in the presence of the master and observing how he did business was a major factor in their stewardship growth.

How can we translate this parable's truths to our businesses today? We can ask questions: What are we reading? Who are we surrounding ourselves with in the workplace? What are we doing to grow and develop ourselves? If what we do proceeds from who we are, then we need to start with ourselves. Better work lives—better businesses—begin with us becoming better.

THE WISDOM OF ADDING VALUE

When the two faithful stewards added value, the master was pleased. He affirmed and congratulated the stewards, calling them faithful and trustworthy. However, for the servant who went and hid his talent out of fear and laziness, the master had harsh words. He called the servant wicked and slothful. This servant had been disobedient to what he had learned. For not implementing the lessons that his master had exemplified, he was cast out—fired from the company.

Several years back, the World Economic Forum, in its "Future of Jobs" report, outlined the top 10 skills that would be necessary for working individuals in 2020. This list included:

1. complex problem solving
2. critical thinking
3. creativity
4. people management
5. coordinating with others
6. emotional intelligence
7. judgment and decision making
8. service orientation
9. negotiation
10. cognitive flexibility.[15]

I venture to say these skill sets are essential for the fivefold commands we've already covered: being fruitful, multiplying, replenishing, subduing, and having dominion over industries and markets. In the

15. Alex Gray, "The Ten Skills You Need to Thrive in the Fourth Industrial Revolutions," January 19, 2016, *https://www.weforum. org/agenda/2016/01/the-10-skills-you-need-to-thrive-in-the-fourth- industrial-revolution.*

above-mentioned parable, the stewards had to have some of these skills too. Let's look at just a few.

Critical Thinking. These servants had the ability to objectively review, organize, and analyze thoughts and resources into intentional strategies for efficient and effective implementation.

Resourcefulness. The servants needed to be clever and quick when unfavorable decisions didn't result in the desired outcome. Maybe they had to choose alternative strategies to meet their goals.

Creativity. Rarely does the best option fall in front of us. Instead, these servants had to find fresh ways to do things. Perhaps they tried things no one else had attempted before. Maybe they combined strategies and created a new business model. Regardless of what they did, the absence of their master meant they were left to their own devices.

The stewards were entrepreneurs and responsible for devising a plan to maximize the master's return on investment. Remember the two words from the Hebrew that mean "to make something from nothing" and "to make something from something that already exists"? This is what the marketplace is all about. Ideas and concepts of innovation are built one upon another. Today's latest cellular phone model was simply built upon the last.

I'm sure we could go on and on, but for the sake of time, let's quickly mention their need for emotional intelligence. These servants needed cultural sensitivity and awareness; they had to understand the viewpoints of people, whether those people agreed with their own strategies or not. They had to understand the personal and professional aspects of doing business. They had to be flexible. This doesn't mean they compromised their values but that they were willing to modify and adapt their approach depending on what a certain situation required.

Alvin Toffler puts it this way: "The illiterate of the twenty-first century will not be those who cannot read and write but those who cannot learn, unlearn, and relearn." The faithful servants were willing to unlearn and relearn, implementing their master's characteristics in situations unique to their own endeavors. They maintained integrity and found new ways of doing business at the same time.

THE NEED TO BE ACCOUNTABLE

We see that, at the very least, the master expected the stewards to delegate the talents to a third party for interest. In other words, they had the option of letting the money work for them in a passive way. However, the servant with one talent didn't even do this much.

The unfaithful steward accused the master of being too harsh in demanding an account of what he had entrusted to the servant. What gall he had! The talent had never even been his—it was the master's. It's as if the servant was demeaning the master's character based on his own lack of responsibility.

Have you ever experienced something like this in the marketplace? Have people defamed your character when you shined a light on their lack of diligence or growth? People try to defame, blame, and railroad you out. We see that this same thing happens in the Bible. Just look at Cain and Abel! Instead of competing, we need to learn how to complement each other—how to work together to learn and grow. It's likely that the two faithful servants did just this, working together to support one another in their stewardship efforts for the master.

To conclude, we can see the values of the master in the actions of the stewards. The master wanted honesty, diligence, discipline, and hard work, and he expected them to be accountable to their responsibilities. The principle we find here is that each person has ability, and with ability comes responsibility, and with responsibility comes accountability. For every ability you have, you are accountable how you respond to it. We'll answer one day to God for whether or not we served our communities—our world—with the gifts we've been given.

THE PRINCIPLE OF MANAGEMENT

In the story of the talents, promotion to the next level of entrustment was dependent upon the management of talents given at the previous level. So, too, your growth is dependent upon your ability to develop your management skills here and now.

Early in my own business journey, I often wondered why some people became rich and others remained poor. I learned along the way that much of this is because of how people choose to manage their resources. Part of management is education. If people are not taught, how can they learn? If they don't learn, how can they earn? If they cannot earn, how can they acquire? And if they cannot acquire, how can they desire to help others do the same? It's a cycle.

I also wondered why people who already had wealth received more wealth. Again, this is due to the principle of management. Resources are attracted to management. Have you seen the show *Shark Tank*? Some of the most successful experts in the business world field pitches from up-and-coming entrepreneurs and provide support based on the potential they see in the ideas. Invariably, the professionals ask the new businesspeople about their concepts, content, and investments, as well as the outcomes that have already resulted before the present meeting. The sharks are looking for management. When they hear certain details, they understand the present level of the entrepreneur's management and can anticipate the future of the business if more resources are added.

If we don't manage the resources and learning we have at one level, we will not advance to the next. We see, then, that management permeates every area of life. Management is all around us every day; we simply don't often recognize it.

Let's go back to creation. God created day and night, sky and water, field and land. He created man, in part, to manage the resources that He placed above, upon, and within the ground. The deeper man would search to find resources, the greater the value he would find. The deeper you go into the earth, the more valuable the resources you find. Similarly, the deeper you go into man, the more hidden treasure you find. Only deep within us do we find our spirit, our being—our connection to the eternal Creator of all living things.

We have a responsibility to our Maker not only to explore and steward the resources outside of ourselves, but to cultivate, keep healthy, and multiply the resources we find buried inside of ourselves, too. Only then will we be full-fledged stewards, able to manage well and take on more and more for His glory.

Chapter 5

SHIFT YOUR PERSPECTIVE

We are a masterpiece of the Master, so we should have mastery over what He gave us. —Dr. Cindy Trimm

People often ask me what the most expensive property in the world is. In answer to this question, my mentor would often say, "The graveyard, because this is where books, ideas, cures, and artwork lie that were never released to the world." While I agree that these contributions are missed opportunities for humanity, I'd like to think for a moment on property that cannot be seen with the naked eye. You can't see it, but you see the results of it.

This is something we've already talked about. Remember what God did after He formed the structure of man? He created intellectual property. God breathed His nature and character into man—His intellect and innovative nature. The power of intellectual property can be seen throughout creation. What God envisioned, He formed and fashioned into vision. The intangible became tangible. The most powerful force and richest bedrock of wealth was found within man's ability to think.

Intellectual property is expansive yet limiting; it is creative, and yet it can be destructive; it is intangible, yet it brings forth the tangible. It is within itself a paradox that governs and guides the life of man.

In this chapter, we'll study the importance of changing our thinking. Before we can increase our management capabilities and go about our enterprises successfully, we need a shift in thinking. Thinking is the starting point of every solution, every perspective, and every endeavor. Therefore, it makes sense for us to start here.

BE A THERMOSTAT

Recently I was involved in a study on the value of life. The study tested the morality of whose life matters more. We were trying to determine who deserved to live or die, based on the limited amount of treatments and the patients who would need them. I came to a personal conclusion, and my group came to a consensus a bit different from mine.

Little did I know that the reaction given by the facilitator would raise the temperature of the room. I decided, despite the atmosphere, to be a thermostat. You see, a thermostat decides the temperature of the room and doesn't deter from it, regardless of the pressure placed upon it. The wisest man who ever lived said it this way: "A soft answer turneth away wrath: but grievous words stir up anger. The tongue of the wise useth knowledge aright: but the mouth of fools poureth out foolishness" (Proverbs 15:1, KJV).

I knew that raising the temperature of the environment would only add fuel to the fire, so I chose not to react and instead listened. It turned out, in the end, that the facilitator had purposefully raised the temperature in order to test my ability to remain composed. I had passed the test because I remembered the time-tested principles I'd been taught. I had shifted my thinking, and my outcome had changed because of it.

CHANGE YOUR THINKING

This is why the Bible tells us to change our thinking—namely, to repent. Thinking affects every part of one's inner environment and, eventually, one's outer entombment. Proverbs 23:7 (KJV) explains, "For as he thinketh in his heart, so is he." Thinking dictates what a man becomes, and it starts in his inner sanctum. If you want to know a man's thoughts, watch his actions, because a man becomes his thoughts.

Our thinking is both conscious and subconscious. We take in information consciously, but that same information enters into the subconscious. Based on subconscious thought, we decide whether to agree with the information or to disagree with it. Thinking forms our individual ideas, and it also makes it possible for people to come together and form groups, communities, and governments based on similar shared ideas. This is the power of thinking and intellect. This is also why the ancient text tells us to think on pure, just, and lovely things and to renew our minds. We are encouraged to associate with like-minded people and those who propel us to stretch our thinking. It is through our thoughts that we change the trajectory of our lives and, ultimately, our world.

For many years, my parents had my siblings and me attend the Harrison International Events, which were held in Florida, California, and Hawaii. You could probably guess that Hawaii was my favorite location, but I digress. These events, hosted by Dr. Bob Harrison, brought together leaders and influencers from around the world who shared their insights on business and personal development and growth. During one of the events, Dr. Harrison shared a powerful truth drawn from Hosea 4:6: "People are destroyed from a lack of knowledge." He went on to tell of the minority ownership he had in a car dealership that needed an overhaul for its survival. With the knowledge he had from business training and time-tested principles, he began incorporating necessary changes, which ranged from retraining the salespersons and improving dealership standards and protocols, all the way to maintaining beautiful landscaping. Dr. Harrison's knowledge led to the car dealership being one of the top producers nationwide.

Change is neither easy nor comfortable. But nothing happens or changes without someone who becomes the catalyst of that change. Change begins in our minds. Like Dr. Harrison's story shows, the way to make change is to become the change.

THE FIVE CAPITALS MODEL

We have seen from the beginning that the Creator is an entrepreneur—creating and assessing resources, developing and analyzing environments, creating products from resources, and establishing systems of management, sustainability, and growth by distribution and multiplication. All of the aforementioned are examples of the Five Capitals Model, expounded upon by the Forum for the Future.[16]

_____

16. See *https://www.forumforthefuture.org/the-five-capitals*.

The Five Capitals Model outlines the five capitals of enterprise and society, which are natural capital, human capital, social capital, manufactured capital, and financial capital. I want to show you how this model can help us in our leadership and stewardship journeys.

First, let's define *capital*. Capital is "wealth in the form of money or other assets owned by a person or organization or available or contributed for a particular purpose such as starting a company or investing."[17] The Five Capitals Model introduces us to the main forms of capital in our world and how each one affects our lives. Let's look at each one in turn.

1. Natural Capital

The first kind of capital is natural capital. These are raw resources—those that occur naturally, so aren't made by humans. In Genesis 1–2, God shows and tells man where the waters, earth, flora, and fauna reside. God gave man the natural resources he would need in order to sustain and advance his environment.

Everything man has created has come from the original natural resources God made. A table comes from wood, or minerals, made by God. Even synthetic things come from some derivative of what God made. If we look closer at Genesis 2, we see the order in which God

---

17. *Lexico*, s.v. "capital," accessed June 14, 2020, *https://www.lexico.com/en/definition/capital*.

introduced man to the natural resources of Eden. We must remember that God is a god of order and protocol. He does not do or say things haphazardly. He is always intentional.

In Genesis 2:9 (NIV), God causes trees to grow that are "pleasing to the eye and good for food." There are also two additional trees—one of life and one of knowledge and the ability to discern good versus evil. One would suppose that man would rely on life and knowledge in order to survive, as well as the understanding of what is beneficial and what is harmful to him. Then God created rivers, which divided other natural elements that are distinctly mentioned in order—gold, resin, and onyx. It is from these elements that man has evolved currency, wealth, and adornments. Trees for food and rivers for water are the first natural resources mentioned, and also are those that sustain mankind. Man, being formed from the earth, needs those things which grow from and come from the earth in order to live. Here we see that God is an agriculturalist and horticulturalist. These natural resources are necessary for the development and maintenance of humanity. These are all-natural capital.

2. Human Capital

Whatever your style, whatever your method, you need to believe in yourself, your ideas and your staff. Nobody

can be successful alone and you cannot be a great leader
without great people to lead. —*Richard Branson*[18]

Human capital includes the health, knowledge, skills, education, and training of mankind. Human capital also includes the management of innate abilities, discovered talents, and extraordinary giftings. The prowess to harness human capital is carefully and internationally studied in varying sciences, including psychology and physiology. It also relates to our business practices. Human capital is the most labor-intensive and extensive form of capital because it often involves learning and unlearning parts of your ideology as you develop.

Human capital is the change agent for innovation and creativity and the catalyst that affects social, manufactured, and financial capital. Natural capital will lie dormant without humans, and other capital would not exist without humans. When you look at history, you will see that innovations, discoveries, technological advancements, revolutions in government, and even changes in poverty are human-led. When change and ingenuity is needed, there will always be the need for human capital.

The question for business is this: How do we leverage human capital? How does one access the potential capacity within each human? With each individual being

18. Robert Half, "Nine Leadership Skills from Sir Richard Branson," April 24, 2018, *https://www.roberthalf.ae/advice/people-management/9-leadership-skills-sir-richard-branson.*

decidedly unique and at varying levels of skill, education, and access to opportunity, how does one place a value on an individual? This is a task often left to managers, which we will discuss in greater depth later.

3. Social Capital

The third form of capital is the fulcrum of the Five Capitals Model because in it lives the institutions that mold human capital, government, and justice. Social capital is where shared values and morals and a sense of purpose are developed, both individually and collectively. It affects matters both local and global. This is the molder of the mental clay; it is the pen upon the *tabula rasa*. Here is the vital indoctrination of thought, precepts, concepts, and belief systems. Social capital is where reason and logic define acceptable and deplorable behaviors and social norms. God kept it simple: Walk with Him and receive insight and instruction.

Social capital is the accumulation of individual mantras into a collective idea. Society's laws reflect what is considered acceptable for life, lifestyle, and culture. Establishments like government, education centers, religious institutions, and families are a part of social capital. Each of these should provide the proper environment for both the individual and the collective to flourish.

In the recent unrest in Missouri, where a young African-American man by the name of Michael Brown was killed, further examination found that there were no sustainable working places, access to banking institutions, or education standards that would have led to the growth and development of that community. This is not an excuse for the actions that took place but rather a demonstration of what happens when social capital is not ensuring a proper environment for its citizens. Understanding the intricacies of what upholds a community, and that the community upholds the state, is fundamental to understanding culture.

4. Manufactured Capital

It is said, "If you want to know the vision of a nation, watch the roads it builds." Manufactured capital is what is produced from natural capital; it includes things such as chairs and tables made from wood or metal. It is where raw materials contribute to the production process—such as infrastructure technology, etiquette tools, and so on. It is also the value added to the production and development of natural capital. Manufactured capital depends on human capital, and the success and advancement of innovation and creativity depend on the level of education and engagement of those involved. This requires the proper environment that allows people to be productive, relevant, and reciprocal in their work, with the result of positive ingenuity and effect. Manufactured capital adds value to raw materials and also increases the price for the finished product.

Take cotton as an example. Cotton in its raw form is worth a certain amount, but when it is processed, dyed, and made into clothing, its value increases—and so does its price. Humans increase the value of products and services as they increase their own personal value: through innovation, creativity, and design.

5. Financial Capital

Last on the list is financial capital. Financial capital includes shares, bank notes, and bonds. Many times people start with this capital in order to determine what they can afford and manage from the other four capitals, especially since they often lack this in the initial stages of their enterprises and are looking to find it. However, if one outlines the other four types of capital, this one will come.

People often think they can't start because they have no money. However, if you look closely, you'll see that the first capital that must be worked is intellectual capital. Remember the order: *Think. Innovate. Create.* Without thought, none of the other capitals will matter. The initial capital of intellect is what leads to all the others.

TEN KEYS TO SHIFTING YOUR PERSPECTIVE

Too many times we focus our perspective on things outside of ourselves and outside of our control. We look to people and systems around us to determine what we can and should do. While these things can assist us in achieving our end result, they are not the end-all. They are simply part of the journey. What we see when we look outside and around ourselves is determined by how we see ourselves within.

The eyes are the portals of the soul—one's mind, will, and emotions. It's from our soul that we forge our ideology, make decisions, and act. I've learned never to ask people what they think; instead, I look at their actions. The outside gives us an idea of what we can change or improve upon. What are you passionate about improving? What catches your attention? What do you want to change most? It is these things that reveal our purpose to us.

For me, that passion is directed toward promoting education, creating understanding, and promulgating wisdom, in order to engage access. In order to be able to do these things, though—in order to make the most of all the capital at my disposal to better the world around me—I need to first shift my perspective. So, let's look inward and pay attention to our character, our thoughts, the inner workings of our beings. Here are ten helpful keys I've found to forming a healthy perspective.

1. Work on you. The greatest investment you can make is in yourself. Spend time developing who you are. This isn't just for yourself but also for others. Neither is self-work done by yourself; you'll always need others to come alongside you, offer feedback, and give encouragement.

2. Learning grows you. When you learn, you change. When you change, you change the world around you. Always keep learning.

3. Control the things in your control. Your sphere of control is a creative space for you to innovate. Likewise, those things not in your control are not in your creative sphere of influence. Determining what's in your control and learning how to creatively influence it is a lifelong endeavor.

4. Your past is behind you. The present is now. The future is a gift. Don't focus on your past so much that you lose sight of the present and the future.

5. Kindness is not weakness. Of all the things in life you can become, choose to be kind. The world needs more kindness, and it's an art that's developed through practice.

6. Remain humble. Humility is confidence in who you are paired with the understanding that how others may perceive you is the narrative they write about you— not the pen with which you have written your own.

7. Remain human. No matter what highs or lows life's journey takes you through, enjoy, laugh, learn, succeed, fail, hope, love, give... repeat.

8. You will not succeed alone. Honor everyone who comes into your path—even those who burned bridges and closed doors. People are the most valuable part of your journey, so treat them with respect always.

9. Travel outside of your world. Leave your neighborhood, your city, your state, and your country. See the world, even if only through a book or a film or social media. Life is a collage. Partake in experiences of all kinds.

10. Thinking, creating, and innovating are innate. You're already doing all three, even if you don't realize it. Pay attention to your thinking. Create something new. Innovate in your sphere. Always be willing to try new things.

What God thought, or envisioned, was made manifest in creation. He has the perfect perspective, and out of this He was able to manifest His vision on the earth. Out of a healthy perspective, we also envision and create vision.

PAY ATTENTION TO PERCEPTION

I was recently asked to consult on a project of global scope. The group had launched an initiative it felt would easily garner financial support, as its first project had been met with success. However, the stakeholders in this project were at higher levels of influence. When the group members came to me, their disappointment at the lack of buy-in was evident. We couldn't rely on the traditional method of funding and support. We needed to shift our perspective. The end result proved positive, but more importantly, I learned something in the process: Things begin with how we perceive them. How we perceive something is how we believe it. How we believe it is how we receive. And how we receive is how we conceive. Everything starts with perception.

We had to shift how we were perceiving this stalemate. We could view it as stalemate or as an opportunity to think, innovate, and create. We had to remain positive, not looking solely at the negative. We didn't ignore the negative; we simply chose to use it as a stone upon which to step and ascend to the high ground of thought and collaboration. Our perspective had changed.

Notice that in the middle of the word *perspective* is the word *spec*. Spectacle glasses help one to see properly, and spectacles have two main parts: the lenses and the frames. You need the lenses to bring objects into focus, but you also need the frames that hold the lenses in place. This is the power of perspective. What we perceive, we receive as truth. These truths become embedded into our beliefs, and from our beliefs, action emanates.

BEGIN WITHIN

How do we determine if we need glasses? We don't until we are tested by an ophthalmologist.

I remember the day I discovered I needed glasses. I was sitting in class. As the teacher began writing on the board, I found myself squinting to make out the letters. I thought maybe it was because of the reflection of the sunlight on the board. I soon realized I needed to have my eyes checked.

The eye doctor performed various tests. One shone a bright light into the inner cornea of my eyes to see if there was any internal obstruction to my vision. The light was so bright, I thought I would be blinded. Then a puff of cool air was blown into each eye to check if glaucoma was evident. When the doctor had me look at the reading eye chart and I couldn't read all the way down to the lines for perfect 20/20 vision, the doctor knew there was something hindering my sight.

"April, I am diagnosing you with myopia," he said. "That means objects far away from you appear blurry."

"What causes this?" I asked.

"It occurs when the shape of your eye causes light rays to refract incorrectly, and images focus in front of your retina instead of on your retina."

"Ugh," I said. "How can we fix it?"

"With surgery."

To fix my poor vision, I would need surgery. This meant the doctor would have to reshape the inner cornea of my eyes.

The work to change our perspective begins from within. We dig into our beliefs—both conscious and subconscious—to find the underlying causes for decisions we have made. Just like I did as a child, we often need a professional or expert opinion—someone who has knowledge and understanding—to help us.

Perspectives can change due to things such as culture, times, trends, and politics. When we look back at the 1700s and 1800s, we see the explosion of colonialism and imperialism. But during the late 1900s and 2000s, the shift has been towards something Giorgos Kallis, an ecological economist, calls *degrowth* and *relocalization*. Degrowth means that attention is given to human and ecological wellbeing. Relocalization means that economic attention and control are given to local communities.

Our society's focus has shifted inward, to fortifying grassroots causes and local communities. We also see this globally; countries have begun to look more toward their own benefit, focusing inward more than on collaboration with others (unless they are of similar origin and location). It's a reflection of the truth we've been exploring in this chapter, that new perspective within oneself has to precede vision and action.

But how do we understand the perspective we should have? What is the standard? The wisest man who ever lived said this in Proverbs 4:5–10 (AMP):

Get [skillful and godly] wisdom! Acquire understanding [actively seek spiritual discernment, mature comprehension, and logical interpretation]! Do not forget nor turn away from the words of my mouth.

Do not turn away from her (Wisdom) and she will guard and protect you; love her, and she will watch over you.

The beginning of wisdom is: Get [skillful and godly] wisdom [it is preeminent]! And with all your acquiring, get understanding [actively seek spiritual discernment, mature comprehension, and logical interpretation].

Prize wisdom [and exalt her], and she will exalt you; she will honor you if you embrace her.

She shall place on your head a garland of grace; she will present you with a crown of beauty and glory.

Hear, my son, and accept my sayings, and the years of your life will be many.

In the end, new perspective comes from wisdom. Wisdom is the application of knowledge, and it leads to what we're going to talk about in the next chapter: vision. Once your perspective has changed—you know who you are, and you see yourself accordingly—it's time to turn that perspective into concrete vision.

Chapter 6

LET'S TALK VISION

Great minds discuss ideas. Average minds discuss events. Small minds discuss people. —Eleanor Roosevelt

What we see is a result of what people have envisioned. You may be thinking, *Wait a minute. No one envisions him or herself in poverty, hungry, or living under a bridge.* You're right. I'm not saying those in poverty envisioned that for themselves. However, when a person has no vision, according to Proverbs 29:18, that person perishes. They won't become who they are meant to be. They won't discover the special gift placed inside of them.

Vision protects purpose. Vision chooses direction. Vision provides discipline. Vision fuels passion. Vision determines relationships and associations. Vision is what is seen within and manifested without. Vision is the ability to see beyond the present and into the future.

Habakkuk 2:2 admonishes the prophet to write down the vision and make it plain on tablets so that a herald may run with it. Who gives the vision? God does. Who makes it plain? We do.

Making the vision plain can be daunting. It will require honesty, resources, and time. Are you willing to invest the energy into making your dream a reality? In writing this book, I had to determine within myself that the satisfaction of a finished manuscript would outweigh the sleepless nights, the unattended functions, the lost opportunity to watch new Netflix releases, even the delayed relaxation of holiday travel it would require. I knew that if I put the time in for a specified season and committed myself to working on my vision at least an hour or two each day, I would see the end. And that is what I decided to do.

In order to have vision, we need detailed, specific plans. These plans should be PURE—Positive, Understood (by you and others), Relevant (to demand and time), and Ethical (within moral and legal boundaries). In her book *Command Your Morning*, Dr. Cindy Trimm states, "You are the architect and building contractor of your future." What you imagine in your mind will happen in time. Each of us has individual visions and dreams. What are you imagining? What price are you willing to pay? How much time and effort are you willing to invest? The answers will differ for each of us. I can attest to the truth that the bigger the investment, the bigger the return almost always is.

THE IMPORTANCE OF ENVIRONMENT

When someone doesn't have vision, he or she relinquishes the innovation and resourcefulness and creativity that lies within. This may sound harsh, but the resourcefulness of humanity can be found in any situation, any circumstance, any walk of life. For instance, someone thought of using a cardboard box to make a shelter, a shopping cart to transport a few belongings, and even signs to express lack of funds or a job. Even in the simplest terms, ingenuity and innovation can be used.

This is why we must have a proper working environment in which to work out our giftings. The first thing God did was to create an environment. I am often asked, "How do you create the environment you want?" My answer is that you have to be intentional—a skill that comes through discovery of your identity and purpose.

Environment is the atmosphere in which we think, innovate, and create. The saying goes, "An idle mind is the devil's workshop." I used to wonder what that meant growing up, but I realize the truth of it now. Success is, first of all, an inside job. In the last chapter, we talked about having a shift in perspective. When you discover your purpose and how your abilities support it, you can become relentless in your pursuit of that purpose. An environment facilitates that pursuit and makes it easier for you to remain focused on your goal.

For me, one useful tool for refocusing myself on my purpose is praise and worship music. Worship acknowledges who God is, and praise speaks to what He has done. When I worship and praise, I refocus my perspective on Him and on my purpose. That empowers me to chase the vision He's given me more effectively. Science has proven that music soothes the soul and can also be an igniter of inspiration. Music is powerful. It's universal. Music sets my mood and creates my environment. Music helps me set the thermostat of my inner sanctum.

No matter what may be going on around you, whether you initiated it or not, decide to maintain your composure. Remember that thermostats dictate the temperature. When you see someone who is hot-tempered, it means that person has allowed the temperature of his or her life to be set by others, thus giving others control. Decide that you will set your temperature from within, and watch how you radiate peace and calm and are able to think in the midst of turmoil.

What helps you create and develop your environment? What keeps you focused on your goal?

GET KNOWLEDGE, GET UNDERSTANDING, GET WISDOM

In the beginning, God spoke and commanded light to be. The Hebrew word for *light* means "knowledge." Indeed, the light illuminated what was in the mind of God. This passage also suggests that knowledge is the first thing man needs in order to think, create, and innovate.

The first piece of knowledge people must understand is their identity. The first thing God told Adam was *whose* he was. This is important on many levels. Identity is fundamental to relationship. Relationship is fundamental to life and to community. We see this in our workplaces, as the first thing we're given is a job description. This gives you, as an employee, an identity. In effect, it's who you are—chief executive officer, secretary, manager. From your identity comes your function, which correlates to your purpose. Whenever there is a question as to the identity, one looks at the function, which is derived from the purpose.

Knowledge is information and understanding is comprehension, but wisdom is the application of what you know. It's the test of how much you truly understand. This is where perspective meets vision. Vision takes your new perspective and allows you to implement it—to put it into action.

Proverbs 24:3 says that wisdom builds a house. This means that it's only that which you apply that will manifest or be constructed. Many think success is a secret, but it's simply acquiring information, discerning what's true, and then applying it. That's what leads to innovation. The Hebrew word for *understanding* is *binah*. This word means that wisdom increases and multiplies in an infinite variety of ways; it's increased by use. The more you apply wisdom, the more you gain wisdom.

In 1802, Humphry Davy invented the first electric light. He experimented with electricity and created an electric battery—something no one had been able to do until that moment. When he connected wires to his battery and added a piece of carbon, the carbon glowed, producing light. His invention was known as the electric arc lamp.

Then in 1881, Lewis Latimer patented a method for making carbon filaments, allowing light bulbs to burn for hours instead of just minutes. What was the difference between 1802 and 1881? Knowledge, understanding, and wisdom. The amount of information available was different, so the application of that understanding produced different results.

We see this on many levels still today. Soft lighting, color-changing lights, timers connected to lights—the possibilities have expanded remarkably. Can you imagine what would happen if Humphrey Davy and Lewis Latimer were to see all the variations of lighting available today?

The human brain is extraordinary in its capacity. Most computational neuroscientists tend to estimate human storage capacity somewhere between 10 terabytes and 100 terabytes, though the full spectrum of guesses ranges from 1 terabyte to 2.5 petabytes. (One terabyte is equal to about 1,000 gigabytes or about 1 million megabytes; a petabyte is about 1,000 terabytes.)[19]

This shows the potential the human brain has to learn, comprehend, compute, reason, and remember. With this much brainpower, the words "I can't" are inexcusable.

What great innovators have shown us is that accomplishment is less about ability and more about the willingness to persist in the midst of difficulty. Angela Duckworth and James Gross outline two critical determinants for success: self-control and grit. They say self-control is "the capacity to regulate attention, emotion, and behavior in the presence of temptation." Grit

---

19. Forrest Wickman, "Your Brain's Technical Specs: How Many Megabytes of Data Can the Human Mind Hold?," Slate.com, April 24, 2012, *https://slate.com/technology/2012/04/north-koreas-2-mb-of-knowledge-taunt-how-many-megabytes-does-the-human-brain-hold.html.*

is "the tenacious pursuit of a dominant superordinate goal despite setbacks."[20]

The number of tries to invent the first electric light was about ability, but the success of the invention rested more with the willingness and determination—the grit—of Mr. Davy to keep trying until he succeeded.

HOW TO ENVISION

We have the opportunity to innovate and create something brand new, and it starts with vision. Vision is something that is executed based on what you envision. It's what you see inside your mind that determines your actions and results. But how do we envision in order to create a vision? Here are several concrete steps to get you started.

1. Assess and Analyze

This is the stage where you'll figure out how to utilize the five kinds of capital available to you: natural, human, social, manufactured, and financial. This is where you determine what you have and what you can do. It's self-discovery of a sort. What talents, abilities, and gifts do you have?

---

20. Angela Duckworth and James J. Gross, "Self-Control and Grit: Related by Separate Determinants of Success," *Current Directions in Psychological Science* 23, no. 5 (October 2014): 319–325.

In this phase, initiative is vital. Initiative is the ability to assess and implement things independently to the end of resolving difficulty or improving a situation with a fresh approach. Initiating someone is personal. It's decisive, proactive, and diligent. Initiation is creative and resourceful.

It's vital in this phase to seek counsel as well as initiate things on your own. Proverbs 19:20 (NIV) says, "Listen to advice and accept discipline, and at the end you will be counted among the wise." Others can often make us aware of gifts, limitations, or truths we otherwise wouldn't notice.

Luke 14:28 (NLT) echoes the importance of considering all the variables before beginning the work: "But don't begin until you count the cost. For who would begin construction of a building without first calculating the cost to see if there is enough money to finish it?"

This beginning stage requires that you look inward and outward. You first look inward to determine the following: Who are you? What do you have? Talents, abilities, gifts, knowledge. What can you do? What do you need?

During my days in business school, we were taught to "strengthen our weakness." So, if someone was weak in math, he or she would work hard to be more proficient. Yet in later years, this concept changed to "hire your weakness." In other words, instead of taking countless hours to become dexterous at something where a natural proclivity is not there, simply be knowledgeable but hire an expert. Theories and ideas change as thought changes, and innovative concepts push creativity forward.

Once you have your goals in mind—once you've decided what you can do with what you have—it's time to prioritize them. For this, I like to use the Pareto principle. The Pareto principle, created by Italian economist Vilfredo Pareto in 1906, theorizes that 80 percent of your results will be garnered from 20 percent of your cause. In other words, your efforts should be placed into the 20 percent of your projects and goals that will produce 80 percent of your desired results. Oftentimes we work harder but not smarter. Figure out what the most important 20 percent is—what will yield you the most results—and focus your energies on that.

2. Education

Dr. Martin Luther King, Jr., said, "The function of education is to teach one to think intensively and to think critically. Intelligence plus character—that is the goal of true education." As we learn more about ourselves and our mission, we'll be better equipped to carry it out. This is the phase where you gain understanding of the information you gained in the previous step.

Picture a palm tree. Every palm tree has roots that go down deep and wide to gather nutrients for the trunk, branches, and fruit. As you educate yourself on the mission you've discovered, you'll empower yourself to be able to think, create, and innovate in better ways. You'll carry out your purpose with a sense of context.

If your mandate is a tree, education represents the roots that allow it to flourish.

3. Collaboration

Step one revealed what you have and what you need. For the things you don't have, ask yourself these questions: Where can I get it? Who has it? What will it cost? This is where coalitions, partnerships, and alliances may need to be made.

In 1 Chronicles 12:32 (NRSV), we learn about the sons of Issachar. They are reported to be "men who had understanding of the times, to know what Israel ought to do." This is so important in our day and age, and the best understanding comes from networking with and taking notes from other people.

Do you know the tools of your time? Do you know the resources, connections, and information available to you? This is the age of computers, digital technology, apps, facial recognition, digital currency, and so many more resources. Collaboration is all about maximizing the resources around you and, with them, the potential of your business. So, who do you need to connect with to do this?

History is revolutionary. *Revolution* means "to cause a complete or drastic change." In the human experience, it is difficult to surmise if any revolution has ever been complete, yet we are assured that it has always been drastic, as revolutions have worn at the fabric of human normalcy and comfort from thought to innovation to their implementation.

The First Industrial Revolution was the transition to new manufacturing processes in Europe and the United States from the late 1700s until the mid-1800s. From the late 1800s to the early 1900s, the Second Industrial Revolution dovetailed off the First Industrial Revolution. What began as mainly textiles, steam power, and iron catapulted into railroads, chemical usage, and other forms of energy. These revolutions affected not only the technical aspects of society, but also the socioeconomic and cultural aspects of society. Coal, electricity, and petroleum powered manufacturing plants and brought about new concepts in specialized production and labor function. The steam locomotive, automobile, and airplane transformed mobility, while the telegraph and radio broadened the access of information to thousands. "These technological changes made possible a tremendously increased use of natural resources and the mass production of manufactured goods."[21]

---

21. *Encyclopedia Britannica Online*, s.v. "Industrial Revolution," accessed June 14, 2020, *https://www.britannica.com/event/Industrial-Revolution.*

The Third Industrial Revolution began in the early 1950s. This was called the "digital age," from mainframe and personal computing to the internet of the early 1980s. We see that there was almost 100 years between the Second Industrial Revolution and the Third. Yet once the digital age came about, the next revolution ensued just a little over a decade after its predecessor. The Fourth Revolution, which has been our most recent reality, is a world where individuals move between augmented reality and digital domains with the use of technology to enable and manage their lives. Whatever you need, "There's an app for that" is the common phrase. And now we find ourselves entering the Fifth Revolution: the era of artificial intelligence. This is the level of having technology attempt to think and process information as a human would, of algorithms and smart phones and surfaces, holograms, cloning, and self-driving cars.

Throughout all of these revolutions, and even those that are to come, there is one underlying thread: collaboration. Every revolution has called for collaboration. Again, we're reminded of the African proverb that conveys the need for human connectivity: "If you want to go fast, go alone, but if you want to go far, go together." Yes, there have always been visionaries who saw the future. But there will always be those who come together to engage, promote, and implement the vision.

If you ever see a turtle on a fence, know that he did not get there alone. Collaborations and partnerships and alliances allow one to go farther, and sometimes faster. They allow the economization of resources. Collaboration allows you to conserve and protect resources in order to maximize them. If two small non-profits work with youth after school, pooling their resources could allow for a farther reach and impact than asking the same local pool for them and splitting the resources between them.

In John 15:4–6 (NIV), we find John, the son of a well-to-do fisherman, sharing a parable of Jesus that gives a pragmatic perspective of collaboration and resource-to-source relationship:

"Remain in me, as I also remain in you. No branch can bear fruit by itself; it must remain in the vine. Neither can you bear fruit unless you remain in me.

"I am the vine; you are the branches. If you remain in me and I in you, you will bear much fruit; apart from me you can do nothing. If you do not remain in me, you are like a branch that is thrown away and withers; such branches are picked up, thrown into the fire and burned."

In these verses, we see the importance of remaining attached to the source and utilizing the resources that are provided. We also see that detaching from such a reciprocal relationship can lead to disaster.

Relationships must be reciprocal. There must be an exchange in order to keep life flowing. We breathe in to breathe out. Fish breathe in to breathe out. Rain waters the ground, and the ground grows plants that give back into the atmosphere. Everything was created to give. Humans were created to give. This instinct was given to mankind in creation. Anything that does not give, dies. Exchange is the principle of life. There is no life without exchange.

Even enterprise is designed to give, whether it be a good or service, employment, or an opportunity to develop skills. It gives, the people who work give, and the buyer gives money for the good or service. Everything was designed to give. Enterprise meets a need.

The key to thinking, innovating, and creating is to find a problem. This is often considered the antithesis of what humans want to do. The majority of us don't want to find a problem. We just want our problem fixed— by someone else. Yet we want to be successful and wealthy. Or you may say, "I don't want to be wealthy, I just want to change the world." So, what are you changing the world from? Problems? Exactly. Whether you want to be wealthy or just change the world, you will be looking for problems and how to solve them. Thus, my point.

We should look for problems and how to solve them. In doing so, we are engaging in enterprise. We will be looking to manage resources and capital to solve the problems we discover. And however we choose our return, whether in warm satisfaction or financial accumulation, we will be solving a problem.

4. Implementation

This last step is where assessment, education, and collaboration meld into action. Implementation is execution. *Execution* comes from the French word *exucare*, which means "to carry out the plan to action." It's connected to the word *executive*. What is an executive? A person who the carries out or puts into effect a plan, order, or course of action. Although we often think that only presidents, CEOs, managers, or supervisors—those with titles—are executives, we don't often realize that we are *all* executives.

What makes a good executive? It is a combination of the aforementioned characteristics, plus integrity, passion, humility, patience, and courage with a keen sense of purpose.

As an executive, it is imperative to remember to start with what you know, but don't remain there. You need to gather a team around you that knows more than you do. You come together for a common purpose, a common goal. Teams allow for counsel in various expertise. Proverbs 15:22 (NIV) says, "Plans fail for lack of counsel, but with many advisers they succeed."

God Himself had a plan for implementation. We already saw this demonstrated in the book of Genesis.

What plans God envisioned, He spoke and acted upon. This was execution. Remember that when God breathed into man, He breathed His nature and character into mankind. So, as God plans, we should also plan.

There are many clichés about planning, such as "Proper planning prevents poor performance" and "When one fails to plan, he plans to fail." There are also several scriptures that declare God wants to bless our plans and that He values planning. For example, Jeremiah 29:11 (NIV) says, "'For I know the plans I have for you,' declares the LORD, 'plans to prosper you and not to harm you, plans to give you hope and a future.'" God also promises that when we plan in concert with His plans, He will give us the desires of our heart, plan our steps, and make our steps succeed (Psalm 37:4; Proverbs 16:9). Proverbs 16:3 (NIV) says, "Commit to the LORD whatever you do, and he will establish your plans." And Habakkuk 2:2–3 (NKJV) says:

Write the vision
And make it plain on tablets,
That he may run who reads it.
For the vision is yet for an appointed time;
But at the end it will speak, and it will not lie.
Though it tarries, wait for it;
Because it will surely come,
It will not tarry.

What does this mean for business? Having a plan is vital. Planning is like a map. It shows where you are, where you want to go, and, most importantly, the path to get there. Even in times of uncertainty, you can still utilize your plan and remain keen to discover what problem is arising. While you cannot solve a problem on the same level it was created, you must go to the level of the problem to find the remedy. This is what doctors do. Once you tell them your symptoms, they go to the source, which created the problem, but only to find the proper treatment for the ailment.

Implementation is not just talking about doing something; it is doing that something of which you talk about. Start small. Build up. Conserve and protect resources. Be prudent in the allocation of resources. Be resourceful.

In Acts 1:8 (NIV), Jesus tells His disciples, "But you will receive power when the Holy Spirit comes on you; and you will be my witnesses in Jerusalem and in all Judea and Samaria, and to the ends of the earth." The disciples, we see, are to start in their home area of Jerusalem. When we begin to implement our plans, it's important to start local.

This doesn't necessarily mean starting inside your home, however. It means beginning with what you know. Often people start small. We have grandiose ideas and want to branch out far and wide instead of growing our roots down deep first. Starting local often means putting energy and effort into starting your business, contributing financial equity, training for a position, or studying others who are doing similar things.

While today's technology allows us to take our business abroad, we have to be careful where we begin. You can go offshore, but before you do, you need to be good at navigating your own coastline. The principles of *start local* and *start small* transcend every arena of business. Begin where you are.

THE CYCLE OF SIGNIFICANCE™

I am often asked, "How can I be remembered? What can I do to make the world feel my significance? How do I feel significant?"

I like to refer people to the Cycle of Significance™ as an answer to these questions. The Cycle of Significance™ begins and ends with authenticity, relevance, and reciprocity.

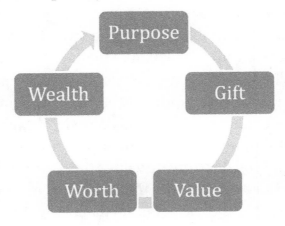

We see several key truths from this cycle:

1. Everything starts with a purpose and is based on that purpose.
2. Your gift is the source of your value.
3. Your gift brings value.
4. Value is determined by the demand for your gift.
5. The demand for your gift is determined by its ability to meet a need or want.
6. The value of the product or service must be relevant to the need.
7. Relevance is key to demand.
8. Demand is vital to wealth.
9. The value you add to a product or service leads to its worth and relevance.
10. Relevance brings significance.
11. Your worth is tied to your significance, and the end result is wealth.
12. Your value determines your worth, and is based on your gifts.
13. Your worth determines your wealth. People will pay for things of worth to them.
14. When we seek to become people of value, we'll find our worth and our wealth multiplying.

In the end, our value equals our significance. So instead of simply seeking wealth, seek to become valuable. What can you do to create value? Promoting your value is important. Recognize the individual responsibility that you have and the potential that lies within you.

When you have a toothache, you look for a dentist that has honed his or her skill and thus added value to their gift. Then because of what that value brings, there is enough worth and significance that you are willing to pay them to fix the pain in your tooth. Reciprocity comes from the service or product that created value, brought wealth, and led to the exchange of wealth, whether that exchange is monetary or in-kind. Wealth comes through relevant significance to the need or desire of another.

After looking at the Cycle of Significance™, you can realize the forging of your vision. Vision is a strategist. Vision gives you the how-to. Vision begins from within and is evidenced without. It creates and designs. It innovates by creating something from nothing and also by adding value to something already in existence through improvement.

Vision begins at the present. It looks at what is present but begins to script a desired outcome. Vision writes the future. It does not regulate itself to the physical limitations of the five senses. Vision is tactical and intentional in its pursuit. It is consumed with passion and discipline. It is driven by conviction of purpose and fueled by inspiration.

Vision knows that to FAIL is simply a First Attempt in Learning. It sees failure as an event and never the individual or the collective. It simply reimagines another tactic to accomplish the strategy.

Vision sees the END as a reminder that Effort Never Dies. It perceives, believes, and conceives different results than someone with no guiding plan.

Vision sees NO as a Next Opportunity. It does not comprehend the word *problem*, and it internalizes opportunities as catalysts for further action and creativity.

Vision keeps the "spec" in perspective. It is perceptive and a bit intuitive. It is thinking and feeling. Vision balances the introvert and the extrovert in you. Vision propels you into the future, into your potential, and into the goal of your desire.

DEVELOP YOUR GIFTS

Refining our skills and releasing our gifts takes time and effort. Both are key to the fulfillment of purpose and the execution of vision.

How do we develop and refine our gifts and skills? In several key ways.

Learn More About It

As we talked about before, learning is one of the most essential factors to maximizing your potential. To get ahead, you must grow your head. This may require investing time and money and going through testing to stretch and grow. This may include schooling, training, finding resources, and many more steps. The greatest investment you can make is in yourself.

Find Mentors, Coaches, and Sponsors

Mentors help by answering specific questions and giving specific advice according to your situation. Coaches, meanwhile, provide overall principles and plans. But the third kind of person you might consider bringing alongside you is a sponsor. Sponsors are willing to put their reputation and access on the line for your patronage. They are willing to promote and champion you. Find all three, and your gifts and skills are sure to flourish.

Develop Your Competency

Developing capacity and knowledge through training is essential. Simply put, the more you practice and use your skills and abilities, the more you'll develop competency, the more your strengths will shine, and the more all of this will become apparent to you and to others.

Embrace Change

Learning to embrace change is foundational to remaining flexible and relevant in whatever enterprise you pursue. You are hired to work. You are hired to produce. And in the world of entrepreneurship, you are expected to create change. I'm constantly investing time and money into learning and growing, both personally and professionally. This is so that I, in turn, can help others discover, release, and maximize their unwrapped gifts and skills.

Bill Gates and Paul Allen are examples of this too. They wanted to create change in the operating system of computer mainframes and developed their skill through the development of Microsoft Office, with programs for writing, computing, reporting, and presenting. They then shared the worth of the operating system they had created. Now it is accessible for every PC and Mac. The wealth that Bill and Paul have received has allowed them to give forward in humanitarian projects related to education and commerce.

Sara Blakely, the founder of Spanx, saw a need based on her own experience and has since fundamentally changed the intimate apparel industry. Forced to wear pantyhose in the hot Floridian climate for her sales role, Blakely disliked the appearance of the seamed foot while wearing open-toed shoes but liked the way the control-top model eliminated panty lines and made her body appear firmer. She experimented cutting off the feet of her pantyhose while wearing them under a new pair of slacks and liked the result. Then she researched how to keep the bottom of the hosiery from rolling up. Thus, Spanx was born.

Often innovation comes from thinking through a product or service that already exists and simply looking at how to add more value to the product to make it more relevant to a specific need. What Sara saw was the need for an undergarment that would give smooth and comfortable support beneath women's clothing. Spanx now has a men's product line as well.

To sum it all up, Proverbs 1:5 (AMP) states, "The wise will hear and increase their learning, and the person of understanding will acquire wise counsel and the skill [to steer his course wisely and lead others to the truth]." Knowledge, wisdom, and vision all increase when we use them. Success is no accident. It is hard work, perseverance, learning, studying, sacrifice, and, most of all, the love of what you are doing. Success is fulfilling the purpose of your unique creation.

Chapter 7

HOW TO GROW YOUR MANAGEMENT SKILLS

Innovation is the specific instrument of entrepreneurship... the act that endows resources with a new capacity to create wealth. —Peter Drucker

Remember the parable of the talents? The master was concerned with how the stewards would handle his resources, and he held them accountable for the responsibility they had been given. The master was an economist, and he wanted the most out of what he'd entrusted to his servants. Their work was their demonstration of their ability to manage.

Another example of management and organization is found in Matthew 14:13–21 (NIV). We know this story as the feeding of the five thousand. Let's read the account together:

> When Jesus heard what had happened, he withdrew by boat privately to a solitary place. Hearing of this, the crowds followed him on foot from the towns. When Jesus landed and saw a large crowd, he had compassion on them and healed their sick.
>
> As evening approached, the disciples came to him and said, "This is a remote place, and it's already getting late. Send the crowds away, so they can go to the villages and buy themselves some food."
>
> Jesus replied, "They do not need to go away. You give them something to eat."
>
> "We have here only five loaves of bread and two fish," they answered.
>
> "Bring them here to me," he said. And he directed the people to sit down on the grass. Taking the five loaves and the two fish and looking up to heaven, he gave thanks and broke the loaves. Then he gave them to the disciples, and the disciples gave them to the people. They all ate and were satisfied, and the disciples picked up twelve basketfuls of broken pieces that were left over. The number of those who ate was about five thousand men, besides women and children.

Jesus was moved with compassion for the people. They didn't want to leave Him, so they stayed into the evening. The disciples knew that their location was remote and suggested that the crowds be sent away to buy food. Jesus told the disciples not to send the people away but to give them something to eat.

As I read this, here is what comes to my mind: The disciples must have had money to feed the people, because Jesus would not have told them that they could feed them otherwise. Perhaps Judas, the treasurer, was being stingy with the finances. Did they think Jesus would send the crowd away hungry? No. So where was their compassion? Maybe you could say they were being practical, but Jesus had commanded them to feed the people. Matthew 6:33 (NIV) says, "But seek first his kingdom and his righteousness, and all these things will be given to you as well." The disciples failed to see that they had the miracle worker with them!

Eventually the disciples went to work, organizing the people into groups, finding the two fish and five loaves, and showing appreciation for the little boy who was willing to sacrifice his lunch to bless others. They began managing the situation.

Then Jesus looked into heaven, to the Source of the resources. We must always remember that thankfulness opens the doors of opportunity. It is a matter of the heart, and as your heart expands in thankfulness, more is added to you.

Then the disciples had to go and pass out the food. Surely they were tired from sitting the people down, looking for food, finding the boy, and taking the food to Jesus. Couldn't Jesus just drop it down from heaven? No. Jesus wanted the disciples to learn several things from this event: organization, appreciation, delegation, and customer service. (Customer service? Yes! The passage says that they all ate and were satisfied.)

Then Jesus taught them what happens with thankful, resourceful management: There are leftovers. The disciples picked up the leftovers—one basket for each of them—and there was no waste. Management, after all, is about efficient and effective allocation of resources to add value. Efficiency is competency and organization working together to have maximum productivity with the least amount of wasted expense and effort. Effectiveness is obtaining the desired result. Management is a concert of efficiency and effectiveness.

FOUR KEYS TO SUCCESSFUL MANAGEMENT

This story provides clear instruction on effective management, delegation, and distribution of resources. These elements are key for business success. This story reflects God's original intent for man—the management of earth's resources. Although you could read this story and see only a tired, hot, hungry crowd and a little boy with a small lunch, there are several keys in this story to unlocking your skill as a successful manager.

1. People will follow what feeds them.

The crowd had been with Jesus all day and was now hungry. There was a problem that needed to be solved. This connects to finding your niche, which is another way of saying that you've found a problem that needs to be solved. People will follow that which feeds them, and they can be fed in body, mind, and soul.

When you look at CEOs, you see problem solvers. I prefer to use the term "opportunity finders." Thinking of these as opportunities instead of crises changes your perspective. When you change the way you see things, you will change the things that you see. You can't solve a problem on the same level it was created; however, you need to go to the level of the problem to find the remedy.

As a leader, CEO, or employee, your job is to provide solutions. This does not mean it must be done single-handedly. It may take the efforts of a team, collaborative, partnership, or collective. Yet the end vision is always before your eyes—the betterment of the company, the individual, and the community.

Your niche discovery will come from identifying problems. Although many try to avoid problems, successful people look for problems to solve. People look for value. That is really all a niche is—a specific way to add value to someone else. What do you have, or what can you create, to give value? What hunger can you feed?

2. If you meet the need, you will reap the seed.

The crowd was isolated, but when Jesus began teaching them and healing them, they grew. Assess the need around you. What talents, abilities, and gifts do you have? If you don't know, ask others around you. People are fairly good at recognizing what others are good at. Ask your family, friends, co-workers, and associates. You will be surprised. The beauty of this deeper search is that we find our strengths and weaknesses and begin to address both. Your talents, abilities, and gifts were given to you for your purpose.

People ask, "Why am I here?" My answer is, "What can you do? What are you good at?" That will give you clues. My mentor Dr. Myles Munroe often said, "You are the answer to a problem in your generation." When you meet that need, you'll see your harvest grow, just like Jesus' crowd grew.

3. The answer is in (the need of) the crowd.

Jesus knew that in such a large crowd, someone had prepared a lunch. He sent the disciples to go and find the answer. This is what leaders do when they create other leaders: They teach by instruction and at the same time know that more is learned by doing. The disciples learned to search and research.

The young boy probably wasn't in the front of the crowd, given the culture of the times. Often we simply look for answers on a surface level. The key to longevity and magnitude of growth is in the deep.

In my first book, *The Calling Card of Business: Success from the Inside Out,* I shared the story of Jesus and Peter's fishing business. Jesus wasn't trying to inconvenience Peter but to get him to shift his location by shifting his thinking. Peter had always done business in a conventional way; God was trying to get him to do the unconventional and reap a greater harvest of fish. Peter was cautious at first and didn't follow the instructions given to him, so he became overwhelmed and had to call for more assistance. But the story ended in overflow and abundance, as happens when one allows heaven to invade one's enterprise. I encourage you to get the book to read more.

4. Get your business in order.

God doesn't bless a mess; He blesses habitations. Remember, God breathed Himself into man only after He created the structure of the man. As such, the disciples must have had a system to feed this crowd.

This is an important key in business—you have to have the proper organizational structure. There are professional legal, financial, business, and risk management advisors that assist with this process. There are also professional organizations and interest groups that provide education, networking, and support systems to start, enhance, and grow your business. Many are at local and governmental levels and can be accessed through websites and followed up with phone calls, emails, and face-to-face meetings. With the internet, there is little excuse to not find what resources you need. And the beauty is that, as you begin to search, you will find assistance and information that is critical to your enterprise.

TEN REQUIRED COMPETENCIES

The business leaders of the twenty-first century will need several competencies to effectively and efficiently address the needs those around them. Let's take a look at ten main competencies for building our management skills.

1. Competence

You must have the skill set necessary to ensure the task is done. This doesn't negate the ability to delegate and manage, but you must have the skill to ascertain and analyze how things need to be done. Those who know this will always be in demand. Learning must be continuous. However, learning also requires action. In the words of Herbert Spencer, "The great aim of education is not knowledge but action."

I work with two global organizations, the International Third World Leadership Association (ITWLA) and Word of Life Ministries (WOLMI), an organization in special consultative status with the United Nations Economic and Social Council (ECOSOC). In both of these organizations, we provide the resources necessary to foster positive change and impact for the communities in which we work. In doing so, it is imperative that we have knowledge about the people we serve: age, gender, ethnicity, resources (natural and value-added), governments, demographics, religious beliefs, levels of education, and so on. All these things need to be known in order for our organizations to determine how to address the opportunities within the nations and organizations in which we work.

Learn about your cause, and never stop learning. You need to determine what skills are necessary to be effective in your field. The internet can assist you in finding the basic core skill sets you need, yet the ever-changing world in which we live will demand that you are always learning, unlearning, and relearning what is new. I think of this in relation to the United Nations. The importance of its existence was determined after the Second World War. Yet the world in which we live presently is no longer the world in which the United Nations was created. Over the years, different agencies and affiliates have been added in order to address the needs and concerns of today. This is a slow wheel turning, yet it is turning nonetheless.

2. Communication

Are you able to communicate effectively? One of the keys to communication is active listening: engaging, showing empathy, and responding accordingly. This takes effort and time.

In his book *Outliers*, Malcolm Gladwell says that it takes 10,000 hours of doing something to truly be an expert. Communication involves understanding the cognitive style of an individual or culture—the way information is organized and processed. How do people in your area of influence communicate? Only once you understand their style of communication and develop effective communication of your own, will you maximize your influence.

Communication skills include your ability to collect and organize information in order to present it in a logical and relevant manner. The presentation could be visual (a PowerPoint or video) or simply a speaker or group of speakers. For those who consider themselves introverts, presenting in front of people may be daunting. It becomes more familiar with learning and a lot of practice. I am not saying you need to be able to speak to a room of 500 people; first, consider if you could talk to a table with 10 or 12 people.

I remember a time I was asked to share on a panel. I admit that although I was a part of a group—and an extrovert—I was still a bit nervous. I felt like the world was watching because we had both a live audience and a livestream, and the panel would also be recorded for the archives.

My mind was full of what ifs, and my stomach was full of butterflies. But then I had a thought: *This is a conversation—a discussion. Instead of talking to the people as if I were presenting, I should talk with the people as if it were a group of us chatting in the living room of a home.* This changed everything for me. When I turned the focus of my presentation to the audience and away from me, much of my apprehension left. At the conclusion of the panel discussion, several people commended me. But I distinctly remember the person who said, "I felt like you were talking with me and not at me."

This is key for business success. Is your business holding a conversation with its stakeholders? The purpose of conversation is to engage in meaningful discussion by the conveyance of the thoughts of all parties involved, in hopes of gaining respect, understanding, honesty, and the desired goal. The attention should be towards the *why* and the *what*. Why are you doing what you're doing? What do you hope to accomplish? Answering these questions will enable you to find the *how* and the *when*.

Companies are the way they are because of why they are. Humanity is the way it is because of why it is. We were created to think, innovate and create. We look for ways to create, discover, and improve our current reality while managing to maximize the resources and capital available to us.

3. Empathy and Emotional Intelligence (EQ)

In today's global marketplace, you need a high EQ. This means the ability to know yourself, recognize the emotions of others, and use this information to guide you in your thinking, behavior, decision making, and negotiations.

An empathic leader is able to sense how others feel and is effective in communicating and building teams and relationships. Emotional intelligence and empathy are also critical in the ability to manage and initiate change. I summarize it this way: Know who you are. Understand who others are. Build a bridge together.

You must also identify the value systems that influence the culture. How are decisions made—individually or collectively? What are the sources of anxiety? What do interpersonal relationships look like? What religions, laws, technologies, and other cultural institutions are present? Are there divisions of power in relation to economics, race, gender, or age?

Emotional intelligence gives you the ability to more smoothly and effectively navigate the culture in which you seek to make a lasting difference. In recent studies by Harvard University, it was found that one of the most vital determinants of the success of a business or negotiation was empathy. Empathy is a component of emotional intelligence. Do you have the ability to walk in the shoes of another?

In cultural awareness training, we explore the extrinsic and intrinsic effects of culture on society, including business dealings, and although we often look at the obvious elements of culture, it is those elements that are intrinsic that generate what is evidenced. As an employee, manager, or CEO, it is imperative that you learn and hone your EQ.

4. Resourcefulness

What can you do with what you have? Are you able to think, innovate, and create? Are you able to engage others with these necessary skill sets? In project management, we call these people *subject matter experts,* or SMEs. An SME has proficiency in his or her subject matter and guides other professionals to ensure the content is accurate.

Part of being resourceful is the ability to access and analyze tangible and intangible attributes and capabilities—what you presently have, what you may need, and how can you obtain what you need. I recall working in a business venture where I needed expertise that would reach beyond my allocated funds. However, I knew that what my company had to offer would be valuable to the company I needed. So, I proposed an exchange: the value of my company's service for the work to be done. In the end, what may have appeared to be an impasse turned into a great working relationship, a long-lasting connection, with referrals from both sides.

There will be instances where you will need to think beyond normal constructs of theory and into creative realms of innovation. That is exactly how humans are wired. We see resourcefulness everywhere, from a brick-laden home to a cardboard-box home to a home created out of sheets and blankets tied together.

5. Soft Skills

In a recent Harvard University study, it was determined that 85 percent of the reason why someone is hired and retained is because of his or her soft skills. These skills are often unlearned. However, as a protocol consultant, I have taught and trained on their importance. Soft skills include honesty, understanding, consideration, etiquette, and protocol. Etiquette is comprised of the guidelines that govern what is perceived as polite or proper behavior. Protocol goes a bit further, into the rules that govern official and ceremonial occasions. The ability to navigate these two areas is invaluable.

My consultancy, The Premiere Image, Inc., specializes in providing the tools necessary to be confident in personal and professional arenas. It never fails. After our trainings, people tell us that the information shared was invaluable. Education is a powerful tool. Once you learn something, it is difficult to unlearn it. But we believe that teaching people to be civil, respectful, considerate, and honest is what fosters goodwill and good governance, both professionally and personally.

When we acknowledge and foster the value of the individual, we see the individual flourish and become more productive. Even the knowledge of which fork to use can help to lower barriers and promote conversational and positive interaction in business.

6. Problem Solving

Problem solving is the ability to access, analyze, surmise, and execute. This helps you not only to find purpose, but also to determine your worth based on the problems you are able to solve with your skill set. All humans have rational thinking and creativity, but what produces a Steve Jobs, a Bill Gates, an Oprah Winfrey, a Sallie Krawcheck, or a Robert Kiyosaki? Problem-solving skills. These skills are developed by learning, exposure, experience, and a lot of personal development and experimental learning.

Problem solving is developing your ability to respond to the issues and the lack right in front of you. For example, Sallie Krawcheck, the founder of Ellevest, decided to "change the money game by disrupting societal expectations that talking about money is 'unladylike' and 'unattractive.'" This is because 86 percent of investment advisors are men, with an average age of fifty or above, and the "gender-neutral" investment industry defaults to men's salaries, men's career paths, and men's preferences and lifespans. She said, "We [women] will talk about money with friends, partners, colleagues, family. We will talk to our daughters and nieces about it. We will talk about it at the dinner table. We will normalize these discussions and thus, collectively, give ourselves the information we need to close our gender money gaps."[22] Krawcheck found the opportunity in what was the problem of education and access of women in financial preparedness.

7. Responsibility and Accountability

Leaders understand that they are accountable for how they utilize what they know. Within the last decade, we have seen a rise in corporate social governance and corporate social responsibility. Corporations need to be honest about how they're operating and utilizing resources. This has led to the concept of "social enterprise"—that one needs to be held accountable and be responsible and think about how one's business affects the well-being of one's community, one's nation, and the world.

This is why God told man to cultivate, govern, guard, and keep the garden, protecting the atmosphere and environment of earth—so it would remain in harmony and be life-giving for humanity. Our world today is holding businesses responsible for their effects on society, but this accountability has been in place from the beginning.

---

22. Sallie Krawcheck, "Let's Disrupt Money," May 4, 2018, Ellevest. com, *https://www.ellevest.com/magazine/disrupt-money/disrupt-money*.

8. Conflict Resolution

There will be conflicts. People do not always see eye to eye. This is good! Yet it is imperative that we're able to come together to discuss differences in healthy ways. Having conflict resolution skills doesn't guarantee you'll solve every conflict. However, these skills can be beneficial in mitigating conflict.

Cultural Intelligence (CI) is the ability to recognize and comprehend the complexity of ideas, emotions, values, and behaviors within a group. Culture affects all dimensions of society, including relationships, information, conflict, and decision making. It's the beliefs, values, assumptions, work styles, management patterns, and other aspects of a community. In conflict, one must be careful of stereotyping and making generalizations. Only by developing conflict resolution skills can we more smoothly navigate the waters of stewardship and management.

9. Strategy and Vision

A leader must be visionary and have the ability to strategically plan for seen and unseen factors. Such factors can include national and international government policies, local and global suppliers, logistics, and human resources, just to name a few.

A leader has to be intentional and deliberate in planning and execution. In Matthew 10:16, Jesus tells His disciples to be wise as serpents yet harmless as doves. The word used for *wise* means "to be sagacious—shrewd; cunning and exacting." This verse tells us that a true leader has both wisdom and restraint.

Undoubtedly, every company expects its leaders to increase profitability, expand market share, and deftly manage and maximize all resources and capitals available to them. In *Seven Transformations of Leadership*, David Rooke and William R. Torbert argue that what makes great leaders is their "action logic—how they interpret their own and others' behavior and how they maintain power or protect against threats."[23] This concept combines emotional intelligence, competency, and strategy into the ethos of leadership. "Action logic" is thus comprised of interpersonal behaviors, relationships, and the interpretation of opportunities to learn.

10. Character

"Character is like a tree and reputation like a shadow. The shadow is what we think of it; the tree is the real thing." —Abraham Lincoln

---

23. David Rooke and William R. Torbert, "Seven Transformations of Leadership," *Harvard Business Review*, April 2005.

Character is the core of every person and every business. Everything a person or business does proceeds from within. In my book *The Calling Card of Business: Success from the Inside Out*, I share insights that my mentors gave me into what pivoted them into success and helped them sustain success. Character was at the top. I thought the biggest secret would be where they attended school, the degree they chose, or perhaps a good investment. One of them said to me, "April, talent and ability may get you to the top, but it is your character that will keep you there." Many of us may recall persons and companies that rose to great fame, only to have their lives sullied in scandal or mired by a poor decision.

The belief in the importance of ethical character is globally evidenced in the "Declaration Toward a Global Ethic" put forth by the Parliament of the World's Religions in 1993, which rests upon two fundamental ethical demands as its foundation: first, the Golden Rule, which says that which you wish done to yourself, do to others; and second, that every human being must be treated humanely. The document further outlines that:

- Every human has equal chance to reach full potential as human beings.
- Earth cannot be changed for the better unless the consciousness of individuals is changed first.

- We must speak and act truthfully, and with compassion, dealing fairly with all.
- We must not steal.[24]

As a leader in the marketplace, one must maintain honest character and conduct business in an ethical manner.

Integrity is a component of character. In the last several decades, we have seen what a lack of character does in the examples of Ponzi schemes, Libor rigging, foreclosures of unprecedented proportions, and the poor education of students in middle and high school.

A leader builds trust by consistently exemplifying competence, connection, and character. Character communicates consistency. Everything around a good leader may be changing—even his own strategy—but his character must remain consistent.

Character is what protects a leader's abilities and gifts. It is his or her personal security system. J. R. Miller said, "The only thing that walks back from the tomb with mourners and refuses to be buried is the character of a man. What a man is survives him. It can never be buried." This quote encapsulates not only the present impact of character but the legacy it leaves behind that transcends generations.

---

24. Parliament of the World's Religions, "Declaration Toward a Global Ethic," September 4, 1993, *https://parliamentofreligions.org/pwr_resources/_includes/FCKcontent/File/TowardsAGlobalEthic.pdf.*

WHAT WILL YOU TRANSFER?

All of the above-mentioned competencies can be learned and improved upon through education and experiential learning application. It's up to us, as leaders, to constantly be developing character and skill sets, so that we're prepared for the purposes and causes we set out to pursue.

Leaders transfer their values into their organizations. Parents transfer their values into their homes. And, communities transfer their values into their nations. The question one must ask is, "What am I transferring, and is it producing the results that I want to see?"

When the disciples found the boy with the lunch, they gave the lunch to Jesus, their Source. Jesus then gave it to God, His Source. This principle should not surprise us. When there is something wrong with a tree, plant, or human, a farmer or doctor goes to the source—the root or the blood, respectively—to determine what to do. Jesus went to His Source and asked for blessing upon that which He had been given—the five loaves and two fish. Afterward, He broke it and gave it to His disciples. In this miracle story, we see organization, resource allocation, appreciation for resources, delegation and logistics, good customer service, and responsible management. We see the need for skill sets and management competency for leaders, no matter their fields.

Now that we've studied how to develop our skills in these areas, let's take a look at some management strategies we can use to maximize our influence.

Chapter 8

BUSINESS MODELS FOR SUCCESS

Instead of worrying about what you cannot control, shift your energy to what you can create. —Roy T. Bennett

was recently asked, "How do you start when you're afraid?" My response was, "You start. But make sure you have done your due diligence in galvanizing the structure of the business. We know that a natural disaster may destroy a structure. However, it takes a lot of strength and power to do so. If you have a strong enough structure, it will be able to withstand the winds and waves that may come toward it. When the foundation is sure, the structure is sound."

In this final chapter, I'll provide you with more biblical and current examples of successful business structures and strategies. You'll learn how to set yourself up for success and be inspired by those who have gone before you. My hope is that you'll gain a sense of inspiration and motivation to implement wise strategies in your enterprise, from the first visionary meeting onward.

BUSINESS MODEL 1: THE ENTREPRENEUR

The entrepreneur always searches for change, responds to it, and exploits it as an opportunity. —Peter F. Drucker

In 2 Kings 4:1–7, we find the story of a widowed woman with two sons. Her sons were to be taken into custody to pay for their father's debt. The verses do not elaborate on the father's debt, but we know it must have been significant enough to warrant the sons being taken away. The husband may have died suddenly before he had an opportunity to pay off the debt, or build an inheritance; regardless, his family was left with the responsibility of the debt.

Sometimes circumstances beyond your control thrust you into survival mode, where you learn resourcefulness. In desperation, the woman went to her husband's former employer, Elisha (He was the lead prophet of the association of prophets.), and reminded him that her husband was in relationship with the organization. She began to recount her present situation, that the creditors were coming. The first thing the prophet Elisha did was ask the woman what was in her house.

If you're like me, you may ask, "What does debt have to do with what's in your house?" Two things: The purchases within the house are what got you into debt, and the selling of the things within the house has the potential to get you out of debt. As the saying goes, "One man's trash is another man's treasure." Elisha's question was meant to redirect the woman's mindset toward finding a solution already within her reach. This is profound and yet simple.

Many times, what we think will take a lot of money, resources, and time doesn't. The solution to your problem lies within you. When we feel we have nothing to give, it's often because we overlook the tangible and intangible things God has given us. What do you have in your home that can generate funds? It could be an idea you've been contemplating, or tangible objects.

The next thing the prophet told the woman shocked me. He told her to go around to all of her neighbors and borrow as many jars as she could find. Why would he tell her to borrow when she was already in debt? Could it be that sometimes, to make money, you have to borrow first? Yes. This is what the prophet was telling her.

The strategy was utilizing what was in her house. The tactic was to borrow and then sell.

But in the middle of all of this, Elisha gave the woman specific instructions, and the specificity of detail is what makes ordinary leaders extraordinary. He told her to go into the house and close the door behind her and begin to pour the oil out. He also told her to involve her sons. Why should her sons work to pay off the debt they didn't help create? Because it is important to work together as a family. They would innovate to create a solution to the problem they faced.

Now, I want to add that these oil pots were not small in size. They were made of clay, so they were heavy. They were deep and narrow, had no handles, and were usually inserted into a stone or wooden stand or into holes in the ground. The top was capped with wood or soft material.

Olive oil was valuable because of its many uses, yet was placed into an earthen vessel. The Bible describes us as possessing treasures in earthen vessels. What was the treasure of the oil pot? The oil itself. The sweat it took to fill it. The price it cost to purchase it. And yet the prophet tells her to borrow and pour—out of her pain and agony—into the empty pots.

You have the answer to somebody else's problem. If you can withstand the shame of borrowing and persevere, you will reap the rewards of your efforts. Do not become weary and give up. Keep working your business; keep going through the process. In due time, you will reap the rewards. On average, this takes about three years for business owners.

The woman's sons brought her all the containers they could find. At this point, we can imagine that her home was quite full. She had exhausted all of her resources to create this opportunity, and now it was time to take it to the next level—distribution. She had been fruitful, using what she had. She had multiplied the number of pots. Now it was time to dominate the market. The prophet told her, "Go, sell the oil and pay your debt, and you and your sons can live on the rest."

The first step was to pay those she owed. We can imagine she had already talked to her creditors to tell them she needed more time but had an idea that would enable her to pay them back. Over and over, this woman's faith was being tested. This is exactly what happens in business. You will be tested on every level. If you remain steadfast, you will see true results.

Do you remember the definition of *entrepreneurship* in the opening of the book? There, I shared that it often begins with using something you already have, or "creating something out of nothing." In this story, the widow woman had oil and a pot. When the prophet gave her instructions on how to pay off her debt, the instructions put a demand on the potential that was in what she possessed—oil and a pot. Both were valuable to her community.

When she began to collaborate (borrow resources) with other pot owners in her community, she found herself in business. This start-up was beneficial to her entire household and led not only to debt relief but also to building a legacy of knowledge and proprietorship.

Often, what we seek to start our business comes from what we have, such as a talent, a tool, or idea.

BUSINESS MODEL 2: THE CORPORATE MODEL

When you see a successful company, know that it took a team to achieve that success, and it will take a team to move forward. Yet the team members may change.
—April Ripley

In chapter 4, we looked at the Parable of the Talents. The faithful servants multiplied what they were given, while the wicked, lazy servant did nothing with his talent.

The word *servant* in that passage comes from a Greek word that means "to have a relationship with; to do business." The phrase *make a profit* comes from a Greek word that means "to manage money to gain interest." The servants were stewards of the master's resources; they were his business partners.

When the master returned for the accounting, their responses evidenced their individual capacity. The master called the productive servants faithful. They were invited into rest and reward for their labors. But the servant who buried his talent was called lazy and slothful—disobedient—and cast into darkness. From this we see that lack of productivity is considered disobedient. When we are given talents—resources of any kind—we are to think, innovate, and create in order to add value to those resources.

In this story we see the corporate-structure model. There is the master (CEO) and stewards (varying employee levels of responsibility, that is, VP, director, manager, and new hire). The expectation of the CEO is profitability (usury, interest), value added to the product, and the well-being of the employees. Each employee had been trained and equipped with what would be needed to ensure success, as is evident in the CEO's response to the new hire knowing the expectations and requirements for the position. We see that the CEO was equitable and just in the expectation and accountability of each employee, given their varied amount of allotted talents. Their earnings and promotion within the organization were clear. Each had been given a job description, which included scope of work, goals, and reporting. For the employees that met their objectives, they were rewarded accordingly (the five-talent and two-talent stewards, respectively). The new hire (the one-talent steward) was not productive, citing the company culture as too demanding and arduous, and was relieved of duty.

This model shows that corporations should have well-defined strategy and goals, tactical training, cohesive company culture, and fair and equitable remuneration.

BUSINESS MODEL 3: THE ACADEMIC

The power of ideas is demonstrated through the inscribed thoughts of men and women throughout the centuries. As the saying goes, "A short pencil is better than a long memory." History has shown the fortitude of words to incite, to calm, and to beguile. The power of concepts and ideas is evidenced in today's academia, from thinkers to playwrights to poets to activists.

A concept is a thought or collection of thoughts. The word is derived from the Latin word *conceptum*, which means "something conceived." Its Latin meaning implies that something is seeded, nurtured, grown, and birthed into a construct—a philosophy. Philosophy—the love of knowledge—is a collection of ideas that acts as a guiding principle for your behavior. So, your life is a product of your philosophy. What ideas have you accepted as truth? Where do these "truths" originate? Family, community, social mores, laws, religious beliefs, friends—these "truths" can be spoken or acted out. We observe, adhere to, or rebel against them.

Words compose thoughts, and thoughts become seeds embedded in the mind—first subconsciously, and then consciously. We begin by doing things "without thinking," and this leads to what we call routine.

Academia has the power to bring about change, revolution, and innovation. This can be seen in the impact of the 95 Theses of Martin Luther, the words "Let them eat cake," the "I Have a Dream" speech by Dr. Martin Luther King, Jr., and many other examples. Academia also has the power to destroy and kill, as evidenced by the atrocities of the annihilation of more than six million Jews in World War II, by the genocides in Rwanda and Cambodia, and by xenophobia, segregation, and femicide. The goal of academia is founded upon knowledge (education) but applied in intentional thought and strategic relevance (wisdom).

Several books of the Bible are penned by the wisest man who lived, King Solomon. Solomon's penchant for observing and listening paved the way for the respect and wealth he accumulated. Solomon recognized that the way to secure his legacy and inheritance was to write what he had learned—to pass it along to the generations to follow. He wrote of the lessons and instructions he received from his father and mother and of his mistakes and learnings. Solomon studied life, and from the lessons he learned he created a new source of wisdom. We still read and learn from his words today. In 1926, George Samuel Clason penned *The Richest*

Man in Babylon, which reflects the sage insights and prophetic warnings about life, business, and society that are found in Solomon's writings.

The lessons we learn in business—the good, the bad, and those that afford us more opportunity to thrive— can be passed down to future generations.

This model evidences the impact and influence of thoughts and ideas in the lives of people and the power of the academician. The Book of Proverbs is not just a journal of memories penned by a young man. It is a chronicle of sage insights to navigate the vicissitudes of life.

Ideas and thoughts can lead to love and peace, or hate and war. What people believe will translate into action. These beliefs, ideologies, are a collection of thoughts, influenced by the words of others. These ideas are lived out in communities, public policies, and laws, all of which govern not only individual nations but also those nations' interactions with other nations.

BUSINESS MODEL 4: THE DISRUPTOR

In Luke 5, we see the disruption of industry. Peter and his crew had been fishing in familiar waters, where it was comfortable, but Jesus wanted to expand Peter. So, He called him to go to a place that was unfamiliar and possibly even a bit uncomfortable. Peter may not have wanted to go there, but after the net-breaking fish catch, he was glad he did. We find the story in Luke 5:3–7 (NIV). Let's take a look at the passage:

He got into one of the boats, the one belonging to Simon, and asked him to put out a little from shore. Then he sat down and taught the people from the boat.

When he had finished speaking, he said to Simon, "Put out into deep water, and let down the nets for a catch."

Simon answered, "Master, we've worked hard all night and haven't caught anything. But because you say so, I will let down the nets."

When they had done so, they caught such a large number of fish that their nets began to break. So, they signaled their partners in the other boat to come and help them, and they came and filled both boats so full that they began to sink.

Jesus' instructions were unconventional: Go out during broad daylight and into deep water (where the fish could obviously see the nets). Peter shares his fatigue and frustration due to the lack of productivity of the night's toil. I am sure we can all attest to how Peter felt and have even fallen prey to how Peter thought: *We've been doing it this way, and it's worked before.* It is easier to look toward the familiar and the comfortable, yet here was a young Jewish rabbi giving instructions to a well-trained and very successful businessman.

This is why the disruptors come: to disrupt our thinking, actions, and results—often improving them. To this end, many companies have begun agile operations, welcomed change, and allowed flexibility in how and when work is done in order to achieve maximum results.

Here is what we observe in Peter:

1. His present method of fishing is not working.
2. He is frustrated and unable to think of additional strategies for catching fish.
3. The person from whom he receives an idea is someone outside of Peter's industry—a rabbi.
4. Because of Peter's respect for the rabbi, he dutifully launches the idea given to him.
5. Peter works from obligation, not conviction.
6. When the idea is successful, Peter cannot contain the result.

Here is what we learn from Peter:

1. Often the strategy that leads to breakthrough results comes from the least likely source.
2. If we are willing to take a risk, it could pay off. After all, what you're doing isn't working, right? So why not try? As the saying goes, "You always miss 100 percent of the shots you don't take."
3. The unconventional can lead to the conventional—and even then, we must be prepared to change when the season calls for it.
4. Frustration paralyzed Peter's ability to think, innovate, and create.

5. Sometimes we need to change location—mentally, physically, or both—to find the "brain rush" of ideas that can propel our business.

6. When we succeed in our endeavors, it benefits not only us, but others as well.

7. Part of the core purpose of business is meeting the needs of others.

We see examples of disruptors in Airbnb and rideshare companies like Uber and Lyft. These organizations looked at present industries and, through thought and innovation, found a convenient way to effectively and efficiently connect with the customer by utilizing present technology to become agile and adaptable. Nowadays the conventional hotel booking process and the conventional ride-share experience have been changed through the convenience of phone apps. Disruptors are often the catalyst of change in companies that have operated in more settled and conventional ways.

BUSINESS MODEL 5: THE STRATEGIC ANALYST

One of the first business consultants in history was Joseph, a man who was not only gifted by God to interpret dreams but also a wise strategic planner whom God used to save Egypt, the largest empire in the world at that time, and its surrounding countries during a period of worldwide famine (see Genesis 37; 39–50). God used the gifts He had instilled in Joseph to make a difference in the marketplace.

The dreams Joseph interpreted were for seven years of plenty, or surplus, that would be followed by seven years of famine, or recession. After Joseph told Pharaoh the meaning of the dreams, Pharaoh also looked to Joseph for a strategic plan on how to mitigate the impending famine (recession). Let's take a look at Genesis 41:33–36 (KJV):

Now therefore let Pharaoh look out a man discreet and wise, and set him over the land of Egypt. Let Pharaoh do this, and let him appoint officers over the land, and take up the fifth part of the land of Egypt in the seven plenteous years. And let them gather all the food of those good years that come, and lay up corn under the hand of Pharaoh, and let them keep food in the cities. And that food shall be for store to the land against the seven years of famine, which shall be in the land of Egypt; that the land perish not through the famine.

During the seven years of abundance, the land brought forth bountifully, as we see in verses 47–49 (BSB):

During those seven years, Joseph collected all the excess food in the land of Egypt and stored it in the cities. In every city he laid up the food from the fields around it. So Joseph stored up grain in such abundance, like the sand of the sea, that he stopped keeping track of it; for it was beyond measure.

Remember the Cycle of Significance™? Joseph's gift substantiated his purpose, which led to his value—interpreting dreams—in relevance to time and future events and brought him promotion and wealth.

Like Joseph, Warren Buffet distinguished himself through his ability to anticipate and manage resources in prosperous (bull market) and recessionary (bear market) times. Buffet's prowess has earned him the moniker "The Oracle of Omaha." Joseph's dexterity earned him a nice home, economic increase, a name change, and political influence (likewise for Buffet).

Warren Buffett, chairman and CEO of Berkshire Hathaway, is someone who demonstrated an affinity for strategic analysis and investments. Buffett started investing money earned by delivering newspapers and recycling glass bottles, and he owned property by the age of fourteen. Through his journey to Wharton School of Business at the University of Pennsylvania, the University of Nebraska, and eventually Columbia Business School, he consistently invested while learning. Influenced by Benjamin Graham's concept of value investing—looking at the intrinsic value of the stock, based on its future earnings power—Buffet said, "Price is what you pay. Value is what you get." He cites the teachings of Graham: "The basic ideas of investing are to look at stocks as business, use the market's fluctuations to your advantage, and seek a margin of safety. That's what Ben Graham taught us. A hundred years from now they will still be the cornerstones of investing." As of July 2019, Buffett's net worth was estimated at $82 billion dollars, making him the third wealthiest person in the world.

Lessons we learn from Warren Buffet:

1. Know your skill set.
2. Hone your skill set.
3. Prepare a plan.
4. Be consistent with your plan.
5. It is not enough to have a plan; you must engage, follow through, and execute your plan.
6. Look beneath the surface (and popular opinion) to find the value and relevance of your plan.
7. Having a defined course of action will keep you focused and disciplined in achieving your goals.
8. Do not be afraid of what others may think of your plan. Listen to their insights, but also be confident in yourself.
9. Talk your strategy over with people at higher levels of achievement. Often we ask those on the same level as us. You are a tree in the forest, so ask the owner of the forest.
10. Don't be afraid to fail. Failure is not you. Failure is simply a plan that did not work, so find another way.

BUSINESS MODEL 6: THE INNOVATOR

In the first 11 verses of John 2, we see innovation in the acceleration of fermentation. The process of fermentation in winemaking turns grape juice into an alcoholic beverage. During fermentation, yeasts transform sugars present in the juice into ethanol and carbon dioxide (as a by-product). The process of fermentation usually takes three to five days. Yet this process is accelerated to take no more than minutes in this passage of scripture (KJV):

And the third day there was a marriage in Cana of Galilee; and the mother of Jesus was there: And both Jesus was called, and his disciples, to the marriage. And when they wanted wine, the mother of Jesus saith unto him, They have no wine. Jesus saith unto her, Woman, what have I to do with thee? mine hour is not yet come. His mother saith unto the servants, Whatsoever he saith unto you, do it. And there were set there six waterpots of stone, after the manner of the purifying of the Jews, containing two or three firkins apiece. Jesus saith unto them, Fill the waterpots with water. And they filled them up to the brim. And he saith unto them, Draw out now, and bear unto the governor of the feast. And they bare it. When the ruler of the feast had tasted the water that was made wine, and knew not whence it was: (but the servants which drew the water knew;) the governor of the feast called the bridegroom, and saith unto him,

Every man at the beginning doth set forth good wine; and when men have well drunk, then that which is worse: but thou hast kept the good wine until now. This beginning of miracles did Jesus in Cana of Galilee, and manifested forth his glory; and his disciples believed on him.

Lessons we learn from this miracle:

1. Problems often become promotions.
2. How you perceive the problem determines how you will respond to it.
3. Understanding the need that a problem creates will help determine its solution.
4. The solution to the problem cannot be solved on the same level on which it was created.
5. To find the solution to a problem, one must go to the level on which the problem was created and see above the problem.
6. When you perceive a problem as an opportunity to bring solutions, you rise to a different level of attention.
7. Your motive in wanting to solve the problem should be honest and integrous.
8. Jesus' motive was not to show off; however, because He solved the problem, the solution showed Him off.
9. Sometimes you may not receive credit or accolades for the problems you solve; however, with honest motive and pureness of heart, your inner

fortitude and spirit grow and mature to new levels of understanding.

Innovation can mean utilizing what already exists to create a new mechanism or platform for a product or service. Much of what we've seen in the ages leading up to the Fourth Revolution have been such innovations. Now we see the collaboration of technology with raw materials and human capital to create new methods for distributing and using existing products and services.

Innovation can also mean accelerating the rate or process by which something occurs, as we saw in the story of the water being turned into wine. There was already a process by which wine was made with water; however, this parable showed that by accelerating the process, shortening the lead time from manufacturing to market, the feasters were elated (feeling that the best wine was saved until last). Two questions emerge: What? and How? How does one determine what needs innovation? And after making that determination, what process will be utilized to ensure success?

When you look at what Jeff Bezos did with Amazon, which began as an online book-selling space that deftly captured information about its purchasers and monitored their buying habits, then grew to become the largest direct sales platform in the world, the only words that can describe it are *innovation* and *disruption*. Although Amazon is not a brick-and-mortar store, it has become the largest online market for everything from groceries to clothing to appliances.

Lessons we learn from Amazon:

1. Sometimes you don't have to invent an entirely new product or service. Sometimes innovation is simply improving what already exists.
2. Assessing and analyzing data can help forge new mechanisms and methods for addressing old problems.
3. Convenience is a driver in business. People want what they want when they want it and how they want it.
4. Bezos leveraged the resources of others and melded them into one platform for efficiency.

When you think of the fact that leather is old cow skin and there are thousands of uses and designs for leather, it causes your mind to start thinking creatively. The concepts of "thinking out of the box" and "breaking the glass ceiling" are man-made. Whoever said there was a box or a ceiling? Both boxes and ceilings are man-made. The possibilities are endless.

USE STRATEGY AND TACTICS

Strategy is the language of battle. Tactics are the language of wars. In enterprise, it is imperative to have both. Strategy is the overall desired outcome, and tactics are what will be employed to obtain it.

In the beginning, the battle was the colonization of earth and the management of earth's resources. The tactic was the creation of mankind with the capacity to think, innovate, and create. The ability to envision, along with the ability to manufacture and produce, was given in the mandate. It is important to understand that the desire to be and to create was placed strategically within mankind, along with the ability to formulate the tactics necessary to accomplish these callings.

The formulation of a strategy and its tactics begins with certain questions:

- What do you envision? What you envision within is what will be seen without.
- What is necessary to get it done?
- Are there people around you who know how to accomplish it?
- Do you need to get further learning?
- Is this something that will require a partnership?
- What comes easily to you? Take inventory. What do you enjoy doing?
- What do you not enjoy?
- What would you like to change?
- Where would this idea work best? Do you need to change locations?
- Are you willing to make the investment of time and money to accomplish this?

Tactics for business enterprises include how you choose to organize your company. The examples of strategies we explored in this chapter have worked for others and may also serve your purpose well.

The strategies we use for developing a business begin with a strong self-concept that one's thoughts and ideas have the potential to make a difference in the world. Often we don't have all of the necessary things we need at the onset of the idea, but vision driven by passion and discipline, combined with proper strategy and a willingness to be adaptable to changes along the way, equals a formula for success.

CONCLUSION

*The world as we have created it is a process of our thinking. It cannot be changed without changing our thinking. —
Albert Einstein*

I n 1975, Bill Bright, founder of Campus Crusade, and Loren Cunningham, founder of Youth with a Mission (YWAM), concluded that to truly transform a nation, there were seven aspects of societal influence to address. These include religion, family, education, government, media, arts and entertainment, and business.

While I won't go into detail on each of them here, it's important to note that each of these areas impacts society. We have the opportunity to speak into our religious institutions; our families; our education systems; our political systems; our news and information sources; our entertainment industry; and our business world.

I am hopeful that from this book you've gleaned helpful insights and wisdom that you're preparing to put into practice. No matter what sphere of influence you find yourself in, it's essential to develop the right way of thinking, a clear vision, and strategies that will help you get the job done.

Understand that you were designed with intention, filled with purpose, gifted with value, and given the ability to create wealth by relevance. Wealth is not just financial wealth but includes all of the five capitals.

I have discovered along my journey to building a global organization with partners across six continents and as a part of international organizations that the most invaluable resource is that of human capital. Without the investment, development, and deployment of people, no business will be successful.

People think. People innovate. People create. You must recognize that every person is wealthy because of what is within him or her. The key to becoming effective is honing your skill and creating value by improving you. Then you'll be able to execute creative implementation and become effective and efficient.

Enterprise leads to realized potential, personal fulfillment, expanded growth, business development, and increased profitability. I like to think of enterprise as entering to receive a prize. What is the prize? It is what you envision. It is your dream. It is beginning a marvelous journey into the unknown with what you believe you know and have known, and the prize is the fruition of everything you dreamed.

YOUR SECURITY DETAIL

We often see security guards around those who have some level of fame or importance. We may think that because we don't have a security team following us around, we don't have our own personal security system. However, every person has his or her own detail. It's called character.

In *The 21 Irrefutable Laws of Leadership* by John Maxwell, the Law of Solid Ground reminds us of the importance of competence and character. Trust is the currency of relationships and communicates consistency and integrity of person and business. Even though circumstances may change, the integrity of the leader and the organization must remain constant.

Character is comprised of the mental and moral qualities unique to each individual. It's made up of beliefs and values. It's your integrity. Greed, which is the mismanagement of resources, often grows out of an unchecked desire for personal gain. Now, I'm not saying we can't seek gain at all, but misappropriating resources merely for the benefit of oneself will ultimately undermine your character, purpose, and business.

The Bible is resplendent with instructions for doing business in a just and ethical manner. Deuteronomy 25:13–16 (AMP) reads:

You shall not have in your bag inaccurate weights, a heavy and a light [so you can cheat others]. You shall not have in your house inaccurate measures, a large and a small. You shall have a perfect (full) and just weight, and a perfect and just measure, so that your days may be long in the land which the LORD your God gives you. For everyone who does such things, everyone who acts unjustly [without personal integrity] is utterly repulsive to the LORD your God.

We can see here that character in business is utmost. In the New Testament, Jesus tells His disciples so in Mark 7:20–23 (AMP):

Whatever comes from [the heart of] a man, that is what defiles and dishonors him. For from within, [that is] out the heart of men, come base and malevolent thoughts and schemes, acts of sexual immorality, thefts, murders, adulteries, acts of greed and covetousness, wickedness, deceit, unrestrained conduct, envy and jealousy, slander and profanity, arrogance and self-righteousness and foolishness (poor judgment). All these evil things [schemes and desires] come from within and defile and dishonor the man.

From the Torah to the New Testament, we see a spotlight on the importance of ethics. The Torah outlines tangible ethical acts, but the New Testaments addresses the intention behind them: the inner character of man. Jesus speaks of the heart—the inner sanctum of man's ideology—and warns of the dangers of the heart being defiled. Corruption from within will produce corruption without. We have seen many companies and persons crumble in the last several decades because of deception and greed.

Proverbs 13:11 (AMP) says, "Wealth obtained by fraud dwindles, but he who gathers gradually by [honest] labor will increase [his riches]."

To reiterate, the Bible does not speak against businesses being profitable or successful, but it does speak to the essential nature of wisdom, being centered in godly character, and understanding the purpose and potential of what you steward. No matter what strategy you employ in your business venture, always go back to God's Word. Only by His wisdom can we shift our thinking, find our vision, employ effective strategies, and discover our true potential.

I pray that as you think, innovate, and create, you discover God's amazing, unique purpose for you. If this purpose includes a business enterprise, I hope this book has equipped you to carry out that calling more effectively so that your innovations will make the world a better place.

Now it's up to you: Think. Innovate. Create!

ABOUT THE AUTHOR

April Ripley is the president and CEO of The Premiere Image, Inc., a company devoted to making protocol and etiquette relevant in today's ever-changing world. April has advised and consulted government officials, corporate executives, business professionals, community leaders, and celebrities.

In addition to consulting, April is a sought-after author and speaker who has carried her expertise to six continents. Her books, *The Calling Card of Business: Success from the Inside Out*, and *Eti-Quick: A Quick Reference Guide to the Basics of Etiquette*, as well as television, radio, and social media appearances, have allowed April to share her insights for exceptional living with an even broader audience.

Dr. Ripley earned a business degree from the University of Georgia and certification as a Corporate Etiquette and International Protocol Consultant from the Protocol School of Washington. She holds diplomatic status with the United Nations through Word of Life Ministries International, a non-governmental organization in special status with the UN's Economic and Social Council. April is a trustee and serves on

THINK. INNOVATE. CREATE.

the Executive Board of the International Third World Leadership Association, founded by the late Dr. Myles Munroe, and works with a number of local and international service organizations and initiatives.

www.aprilripley.com